I Was Just a Man

Jayne and Alan Bicker

Pen Press

First published in Great Britain by Pen Press

All paper used in the printing of this book has been made from
wood grown in managed, sustainable forests.

ISBN: 978-1-78003-570-3

Printed and bound in the UK
Pen Press is an imprint of
Indepenpress Publishing Limited
25 Eastern Place
Brighton
BN2 1GJ

A catalogue record of this book is available from
the British Library

Cover design by Jacqueline Abromeit
Cover illustrations by Jo Lowrie, with our thanks

About the Authors

I am Jayne Bicker, wife of Alan Bicker, and this is the first book that I have written. The fact that it is a transcription of conversations; I do not feel that I have written it as such. This is therefore co-written with Alan.

I am 54 years of age and grew up in London and moved to Suffolk when I was 30. Alan is 61 and grew up in a little village in Suffolk. I met Alan in 2000 in a Spiritualist Church and we married a year later in the same Church that we had met. Since then we have been doing spiritual work, firstly having a spiritual shop, through which we used to run spiritual development groups, workshops and courses, and do readings and healing. At this time Alan was regularly doing his trance mediumship, and has continued to develop this ever since. He can now sit in a trance state for two or three hours at a time, and he doesn't remember anything that has been said or happened.

In 2005 we moved to Cambridgeshire and moved the shop there as well, continuing to do teaching and readings etc. We closed the shop in 2008 and started to work doing readings on the phone for different companies. We now both work for Psychic Today, which is a television company broadcasting on Sky Channel 886.

Jayne and Alan Bicker

Contents

Foreword

I Was Just a Man

After developing Alan's trance mediumship for many years, we were graced with the presence of the spirit of a man called Jesus Christ. For many of us in the small group of people that came together regularly, this was the cherry on top of the cake. Why would such an esteemed spiritual being single out a little group like ours? Well, after a couple of months of visiting us, we were soon to find out why.

At the beginning of the year 2010, during one of his visits, Jesus said that he wanted to ask us all something important. He wanted to know if we would all accept a challenge from him, and he went round and asked each of us individually. After each of us duly agreed to do so, he laughed and said that we were all stupid because we didn't even know what it was that he wanted us to do! This was his lovely sense of humour coming out. We replied that we all agreed, because we trusted him.

The challenge that he had set for us was to write a book about his life and to set the record straight.

It was time for the world to know the truth as he sees it. He knows that there are people who, in their ignorance, will call this the work of the devil, but he wants people to start to think for themselves, instead of believing everything that has been told to them by the Bible and religious leaders. Even the fact that the New Testament was put together hundreds of years after his so-called 'death', should make people question its validity. Why were there many texts that were left out? How accurate were his reported miracles? Was he really the Son of God? Did the religious leaders manipulate the stories to make them sound more incredulous so that we would take notice of them?

All these questions have never been answered by Jesus himself, until now. He knows that this will challenge the religious authorities, because when people start questioning and thinking for themselves, the authorities know they will lose the power and control that they have had for thousands of years.

When people can make their own decisions based on what they feel is correct, it will start to loosen the control of religions. Instead of people living good lives because they fear the consequences the religious leaders have instilled in them, they can live good lives because that is what is in their hearts. When they do wrong they will wrestle with their own consciences, instead of living in fear of hell and damnation.

The message from Jesus is ultimately to love and care for yourself and others in the best way that you can.

Introduction

This book is an account of the life of a simple man who was known as Jesus Christ. It has been done through the trance mediumship of Alan Bicker, with assistance from his wife Jayne, their good friend Margaret Cotton, and several other friends and acquaintances.

What is Trance Mediumship?

It is an altered state of consciousness, where the medium will allow evolved spirit beings to use their physical body. It can vary from being a light trance where the medium is aware of everything that goes on, to the deep trance where they have no knowledge of anything that happens.

Alan's trance mediumship is a deep trance and without doubt, truly amazing to see. He has been developing it for many years and has had many hundreds of spirits come and speak through him, ranging from the famous, such as Churchill, to the little known, such as friends and families of the sitters. Alan doesn't remember anything that happens during the session, in his own words, he says, 'I could have streaked through the streets for all I know!'

Spirits instigated the writing of this book because they felt that it was time now for the world to know the truth. Jesus himself, as you will read, has strong views on the way that religion has gained power and control over people, by using his, and God's name. The religious leaders have given themselves status by their so called 'direct line' to the Supreme Being. As you read, you will get to know the passion of the man and that he is a gentle, loving man with a great sense of humour. From the start he has been insistent that, when he walked the earth, he was just an ordinary man. There was nothing magical about him, unless you call tremendous healing, psychic powers and a wonderful rapport with the spirit world, magic.

The following pages are the transcripts from our conversations with the spirit of Jesus, which have shed light on his life, to give us an insight into the truth behind what really happened to him. We realise that there will be many people who will find this book difficult to accept, possibly due to their deeply entrenched beliefs. However, no one is forced to read it. We sincerely hope the reader will find this book of interest.

Chapter One

The Early Years

'Hello. Good afternoon.'

'Greetings, my friends.'

'Thank you. Welcome and thank you for coming. We've got an idea of things that we'd need to talk about, but we'd also like your input and guidance as well, please.'

'I will try my best, maybe just to give them a brief sketch of what my life was like, what I did and how my life went.'

'You could also talk about the circumstances that caused your life – the behind the scenes, as we would say – because I think that is of great interest because your arrival has been echoed in various literatures, yes.'

'Set in the past there has been much written but it was always many years later.'

'Could we perhaps start with what it was that you wanted to achieve before you came, what your aim was in doing this thing?'

'Just to bring man back to the spiritual side, get them to...love may not be the right word, but get them to understand. Even before I returned, man was very similar to the way he is now. He may have advanced in thousands of years, but he is still as much a war-making megalomaniac as ever.'

'Your choice of venue was important to you, why was that?'

'It was simply an easier place to return, or not to return but to, yes to return.'

'You had been there before?'

'I had walked the earth before, yes.'

'In that particular area?'

'Not in that particular area, no, but other parts of the world.'

'In Atlantis?'

'Yes, and other places. That seemed to be a less populated area so that I could be myself for a few years.'

'Can we talk about your actual coming to this world and the astrological set up? So in other words, the bright star that was to indicate that you had been born. You know, the fact that people came from a long way away for your birth? So how was that formed and brought together?'

'Practise and a lot of hard work from our side! It had been, as you would say, written in the stars anyway. The old Magi had seen it and predicted it many years before I had chosen to return. But again, like many other things, there has been a lot of speculation and bigots have put on things that should not have been.'

'Can you put us right with that? That particular time?'

'In what respect?'

'Well, you said many bigots have put on things so in what way do you mean bigots had put on things?'

'That the Son of God was being born.'

'Right.'

'As I have said to you many times in the past, are you not all sons and daughters of God? So it does not make me any more special than you.'

'So the Magi, or whatever you call them, had perhaps over assessed the significance of your arrival. They deified you, which is obviously something that you did not want because it defeats the purpose of your—'

'That again the Magi, or whichever term of phrase you use for them, had access to knowledge from Atlantis as well, so they had things on their side, and in your modern terms they had a great link, a direct link with the spirit realms and could, I don't mean they could speak to us and speak to the angels, but that is the easiest way that I can explain that one to you. They were, like yourselves – mediums, trance mediums and of course, astrologers.'

'When the three noted people came, there was no collusion between them, was there? It was accidental, well, they all had the same idea at the same time, was that right they didn't correspond with each other before?'

'There was no correspondence between them.'

'Apart from...'

'Meeting, I suppose, two thirds of the way towards Bethlehem at the time.'

'So what was the impetus? Was it what had been told to them by spirit or was it the astrological signs that they were looking for?'

'Both sides.'

'So they all set off at the same time?'

'Again, can I ask, how has it been told how these three great kings turned up?'

'Because there was a particular star that was significant, so that bit was true?'

'Yes, but how did they turn up? All on their own? There were at least 30 or 40 people with them. They would not have travelled thousands of miles on a single camel on their own.'

'Of course not, at least there would have been one spare camel!'

'Of course,' laughter, 'there was quite a caravan and quite a host of people with them as well. Again, they would not have travelled on their own because of robbers and other people seeking to take what was not theirs.'

'May I ask, the caravan and the rest of the people, were they as tuned in to the situation as the kings?'

'No, they were not slaves, but...'

'Like tribesmen?'

'Yes, there to protect them and to cook and cater for the animals, pitch their tents.'

'It wasn't theirs to reason why, really.'

'They were just pleased to go along for the prestige of the trip, maybe.'

'So would that have been like the elders of a Native American Indian tribe where they would listen to the elders?'

'Yes, that is a better way of putting it, thank you.'

'That's all right.'

'Again, these people were not forced, they were basically told, we are going on an adventure, who would like to come? I am not saying those are the words that they used but that is the small principle of how it went.'

'The people that were your parents, who you chose as your parents, is there some reason why you chose them?'

'Because I felt they would be the best ones to look after me in my early life. And again, were they not just plain simple people like yourselves?'

'Yes, and the Immaculate Conception?' Laughter all round.

'I do not think that spirit has managed that one yet!'

'So was Joseph actually your biological father or did he just come to the rescue of Mary?'

'He came to the rescue.'

'Did you know who your biological father was? There are stories about Mary being raped, was that correct?'

'It is correct.'

'And was it a soldier or someone we don't know?'

'It does not matter. My father was Joseph as far as I am concerned. He looked after me and taught me many things and he was the only father I knew.'

'Yes, what about the appearance of the Angel Gabriel, who apparently, according to the scriptures, appeared to tell Mary about the Immaculate Conception and not to worry, that things would be all right? That's roughly what happened?'

'Supposedly.'

'Yes, but did that happen? Or was that what was written when the tale was growing?'

'I am sure, yes. A tale to keep the masses enthralled, I feel.'

'Yes, but the Immaculate Conception has been the theme throughout a lot of mythology and was just sort of slapped onto your case to augment your validity as the only Son of God. Is that right?'

'What better way to control the masses again?'

'Good one. So Archangel Gabriel was a complete myth?'

'Mary may have had divine visions from the angelic realms, but for him to appear and speak to her, again a myth. Again, my friends, do you not see and speak to the angels and have you had one fully materialise for you yet? I do not mock, but you have seen them within your mind and you know they are there. That was the same with my mother. She was, as you would call it in modern-day terms, very mediumistic.'

'And was your father as well?'

'No, he could do it, but he was busy with his work. He would support mother and he would heal and do little things, but he would very rarely tap into, as you call it, his spiritual talents.'

'So he was a healer? He must have been a very compassionate man.'

'He had what you would call a "heart of gold".'

'And were you the first born?'

'And no, I was not born in a stable.' Laughter.

'Where were you born, then?'

'At home.'

'At your home, which was where?'

'Just outside Bethlehem.'

'You should see it now!'

'May I ask one question, it is for all of you? If I was born in a stable in Bethlehem, my parents were there for the annual census, was I put on the census roll?'

'It depends whether they filled it in before or after you were born.'

'They had gone there for the annual census, the census was taking place.'

'So I would say they would put it there, yes.'

'Well, is there any record?'

'It depends on whether or not those records were kept from that time. Are you saying that there are records?'

'This is what I am asking you.'

'Well, I wouldn't know. Yes, the census was in Jerusalem, which was several miles from Bethlehem, so did your birth prevent them from going to the census?'

'No, my birth was after the census. As you know, the census was in December according to what has been written, but I was not born until the February.'

'So your home was actually in Bethlehem, because you said you were born at home, so before you were born, your parents travelled to Jerusalem for the census and then came back again and then you were born. Can I ask how old were your parents when you were born?'

'My mother was 17 and my father was 32.'

'Quite an age difference between them. Would that have been usual in that country at the time?'

'My father, as I have been told, was a single man and my mother had been raped as we have said, by a Roman soldier. She had no one and, of course, she would have been a social outcast and might even have been stoned to death. My father, knowing of her and of her plight and being what he was, stepped into the breach and took her as his wife.'

'Did he know her before, was she of the same—'

'They were of the same village, of the same community, yes.'

'And was that a religious community or was it just a community?'

'Why does everything have to be religious?'

'Well, I was wondering whether…it doesn't have to be and I'm not saying it does, I just wondered whether it was a sect or whether—'

'It was just a normal village like your own and more people like yourselves.'

'And were they of a religion or not?'

'They would have been Hebrews.'

'What was the language spoken in the households? Was it Aramaic or Hebrew?'

'Hebrew, some Aramaic and some Greek.'

'Your mother is standing beside you isn't she, because you are asking her things?'

'We were…I was multi-lingual. We were taught many languages in our schools. As you know, we were, I wouldn't say invaded by traders, but it was always passing trade from many camel trains, so we were lucky to be so, I feel. Sorry, my friend, I did not mean to cut you short.'

'That's fine, that's fine, I just became aware of your mother standing there and you asking her questions and she's lovely. So your father was a carpenter and remained a carpenter and were you considered poor or rich or just in the middle somewhere?'

'We were, I suppose you could say, in the middle. We were not poor but we were not filthy rich. We had a reasonably moderate lifestyle – we were well fed, we were well loved and looked after and there was always food on the table.'

'In modern terms, did you have two donkey carts in the garage?'

'I suppose you could say, yes.'

'I guess that narrows it down. I wanted to ask you, did your father teach you carpentry?'

'Yes, he did.'

'Did you enjoy it?'

'Very much so. He taught me from, I must have been about three, and I used to go into the workshop, as you would call it now, with him.'

'And you plied the same trade. What did your father think when you were constantly going away?'

'It did mystify him to start with, but I feel there may even have been, as you would say in your terms, divine intervention.'

'Yes, but he seemed always imperturbable about it?'

'He knew that my fate was not to be a carpenter like himself, my destiny was for other things, and this is something that he did accept and he even encouraged, very much so.'

'So were you brought up as a special child because of the birth and the emphasis on that? Did you continue to have people coming to see you even as you grew up because of who you were supposed to have been?'

'There were one or two, yes.'

'What sort of people would come? I just wondered how wide the awareness was. You talked about the three kings and their entourage.'

'But the three kings, I do not mean they kept it to themselves, but at the time, who would have listened to them? A similar principle of what we are trying to achieve now. People listened, but many thought they were cuckoo.'

'What is the truth or circumstance around you teaching at the very early age in the temple? Was that the essence of what you were doing? Did you actually go in and talk to the high priests?'

'I did go in and talk to them and question them and—'

'Challenge?'

'That is the word, yes.'

'How did they react?'

'Some of them were very angry as to why such a—'

'Whippersnapper?'

'Yes, that is the word – was questioning. They took it that I was questioning their authority but I was questioning the validity of what they were trying to preach to others.'

'So you were really questioning their authority?'

'Their knowledge, maybe.'

'That's what I meant, questioning the validity. They assumed that you were questioning their authority.'

'Yes. Again as I have said, I had very loving parents who taught me much.'

'Did they worry about you journeying, probably on your own, to the temple?'

'Sometimes they did not know.'

'So you had your own way of playing truant?'

'Yes.'

'How young were you when you first started?'

'Six.'

'How many brothers and sisters did you have? I know you had a brother – I know you had at least one brother. How many brothers and sisters did you have?'

'One of each, a brother and a sister.'

'And your brother was called Joseph, is that right?'

'Yes.'

'And what was your sister's name? Mary?'

'I would say, need you ask? I do not mean to sound impolite.'

'I can't understand about the way all the women seemed to be called Mary. That's right, isn't it?'

'It is the name of the times. Take your modern names now – how many young boys are called David and how many young ladies are called Julia, maybe?'

'It seems to me there was Mother Mary, Mary Magdalene, Mary your sister – everyone called Mary. I find it so strange it means bitter, the name means bitter – I would never have called a child of mine that. I would like to ask a question that is about your mother – I consider it a personal thing, though – I make a lot of images about your mother as represented by the Church and I do it with tongue in cheek. Are there any objections as to what I am doing at that end?'

'From my point of view, none at all.'

'I didn't think there was – bless you. It's meant just as a comment on the religious side of stuff, it's not personal.'

'She is privileged that you are portraying her in the way that you do and thanks you.'

'Thank you.'

'She understands what you are doing and there is no animosity on her behalf and knows you are doing this with no disrespect to her.'

'No, it is really trying to break down the stereotype that we have made of her.'

'She feels you are doing a great task.'

'Good, I will continue to do so.'

'One question about that before we move on. I was wondering when you were a young child and went to the temple and were challenging the received knowledge, were you always aware of your mission and at what age did you become aware of your mission? Did you never forget – as Diana Whatsit would say – was the veil never taken away? Was there always such clear links with the spirits?'

'It was a bit later in life. I must have been about nine, maybe ten, when I realised, as you have said, what my mission in life was, just before I went off to study with a friend, or one of the wise men or great kings, as you have called him.'

'Was it that age to protect you so that you had a normal childhood – or as normal as possible – before… before…'

'Before being dropped in at the deep end, yes.'

'If it was at the age of six, then you were already asking incredibly mature, philosophical questions.'

'Are there not children nowadays who do very similar? They call them prodigies, do they not? There have been many of them over the centuries.'

'Did this make you feel different?'

'How do you mean, my friend?'

'Well, as a child you could be very aware that you didn't fit in in some way. Did it make you feel uneasy?'

'Not in the least, and again it is coming back to the love of my parents, the guidance from my father, the love from my mother.'

'They must have been very special people.'

'They were.'

'So did they, then, have an idea of your mission? Did they have an idea of what their role was and what they were dealing with?'

'I feel they did in the end.'

'In the end, not when you were very young?'

'Not when I was very young. My mother did have, again as you would call, divine inspiration. As I said, she was mediumistic so she was prepared in one way and my father had abilities as well so that he was prepared in another way.'

'There seems to have been a lot of trust in your family, well, who you all were. It sounds really nice. But she must have been aware of the visits from the kings, from the wise men. That must have started her thinking about things as well. Would they have talked to her about it?'

'Yes, but when did they arrive?'

'Not when you were born?'

'I think that would have been more luck than judgement.'

'So how old were you when they arrived?'

'About 18 months to two years.'

'That must have caused quite a lot of turmoil in your surroundings, all these caravans.'

'All these strange people arriving.'

'Maybe they camped outside.'

'They camped outside and discreetly came in.'

'So the fact that there was supposed to be this star that guided them to where you were born, is that not actually true?'

'It did guide them towards me.'

'Yes, but not to when you were born?'

'Not from when?'

'No.'

'It basically arrived with the shepherds.'

'They came when you were born?'

'They were friends of the family who knew mother was pregnant.'

'And they were not aware of anything?'

'They were not aware of anything special but they were just like normal friends in today's terms who hear a friend is pregnant and has just had a baby. What do you do? Knock on the door and you go visit. And this is exactly what they did. And of course there were gifts of two small lambs, because this is all they had. They were not poor, but that is all the gifts that they had at the time and that is what they left with us. So some of the tales are... There is some truth inside the tale, yes.'

'I suppose it's like a pearl where a little grain of truth which gets embellished as time goes on.'

'Yes.'

'So when the wise men came. Did they bring, for instance, the frankincense, myrrh and gold?'

'Yes.'

'So there's another bit of the tale that's true.'

'As you know, myrrh and frankincense was of higher value than gold.'

'Oh, really? I wonder what your mother can have thought with these incredibly wise men with their huge camel trains bringing these amazingly valuable gifts.'

'Like you, I am sure she was quite astounded.'

'When people kept turning up who you didn't know, giving you gifts, she must have been wondering quite what was going on. Well, I would have thought I have a very special being here. I would have known that much. And she must have done, because she was mediumistic anyway, and if she did have a vision of Gabriel, I am sure that would have helped her understand, and your father. Or did he perhaps pretend it wasn't happening and carry on making things?'

'He understood what was happening and I feel he got on with his life and tried to make life for me as normal as possible. And of course there was trading between him and the three kings and repairs of things that they had for themselves. Repair of furniture and help with their tents and other small carpentry work. Again there was trade for the family. Besides the riches of what we had been left by the wise men or the three kings, there was another financial side, or what you would say in your modern terms, there was business for my father's business.'

'In your everyday life, did you have close friends of the same age as you?'

'Two or three, yes.'

'What was their fate? Did you stay in touch with them?'

'I did lose touch after the so-called crucifixion because nobody could know what had happened after that because their lives would have been in serious danger.'

'As you grew, what was their fate?'

'We drifted apart, but we would still meet now and again. I won't say we posted letters as you do in modern times, but we did communicate and we did keep in touch, but again, they did not realise the way that I was.'

'How did they react? Well, they must have seen, you know, how you progressed. Did they say, "Hey, you're doing dangerous stuff", the way friends would?'

'They were quite surprised and amazed that I would go to the synagogue and question the elders, and pose questions to them.'

'Were they religious as such?'

'They had their beliefs and, I would not say I was not brought up to respect the elders, but they were brought up to believe what the elders said was, in your terms, gospel.'

'Yes, to accept.'

'Whereas I was, I suppose, the rebel.'

'So, you were in a gang. Well, it was really very natural, being children.'

'In my younger days we were going round the village, typical children getting into all sorts of mischief.'

'Yes, the literature about you kind of implied that you never set a foot wrong, which always in my mind perpetuated the myth that you're not human.'

'I am not saying we were always in trouble, but typical childhood mischief – throwing stones at somebody's sheep or cow, being cheeky to the local innkeeper and having to run so as not to get a cuff of the ear. That was, even in your modern times, a part of childhood growing up. And yes, I did have scuffed knees and cuts and bruises and got into fights with other children and it was just, I suppose, what you would call a natural childhood. Again, I was not kept to one side because of who I was. I had a normal childhood like you. I presume you had a normal childhood?'

'Tell you later! So did you go to what would be considered a normal school and what age did you start school?'

'I suppose I must have been about six, maybe.'

'And that was just within your village, then, your local village where you lived, so quite a small school, then?'

'All ages, all in the same—'

'In the same class?'

'Yes, for a few hours each day.'

'And were you a good scholar?'

'We were not taught to be scholars.'

'Were you a—'

'A perfect student? No!'

'Were you interested in what you were being taught?'

'Some of it.'

'Was that the bit that related more to life and to spiritual philosophy or the bit that you thought inconsequential so you didn't listen? So you say at the age of nine or ten you remembered, became aware of your mission?'

'I was aware of, not my mission, that may not be the right word to use, but I was aware of what abilities I had. But I was not aware of how I could tap in and use them. This was the time that, I am not saying that my parents packed me off, but I went to live with one of the wise men, one of the three kings.'

'Did something happen then that caused you to be aware?'

'Boredom at school!'

'You had kind of outgrown everything?'

'I suppose if you say it in another term, I had matured early. And, again, using your modern terms, when my friends may have been playing with toy cars and things, I had outgrown them.'

'Did your mother probably recognise that, and when did the invitation from the king come?'

'That was left when they first came to see us. As and when the time is right they will be here, or I will be here to take him under our wing to bring forth his talents.'

'Did your mother or even your father keep in touch in some way? Because I find it very difficult that they let you go.'

'With a stranger? There was communication between them.'

'What sort of distance was involved? Are you talking about a different continent or a different country?'

'A different country.'

'So was it Greece? If not, where was it?'

'It was not far from Greece but—'

'Asia Minor or Turkey?'

'Turkey, that is the one I was thinking of, that I would travel to. Again, in modern terms, I lodged with them, I stayed with them. I would go somewhere for a few weeks to learn and then come back.'

'So it wasn't immensely far?'

'Not from where I was staying with one of the three kings.'

'So can you remember what the name of the king was you were staying with?'

'I cannot remember.'

'And was it a king and a queen, or was it just a king?'

'He may not have been a king as you know kings. He was what I have always seen as a wise man, a man of much knowledge.'

'A wise man and his family?'

'He was wealthy, of course. I feel he may not have been a king, but he was wealthy and they looked after me very well. And, of course, I did go back at times to my parents for breaks as well. It was not five or six years of learning.'

'So when you were staying with this wise man, what did he teach you?'

'His knowledge!'

'What did he teach you, because you said you went away?'

'He taught me what you would call astrology, his knowledge of the stars, his knowledge of the solar system, some divination.'

'And you mentioned that you would go away as well, what was that for?'

'I went to Greece to learn Hebrew and to polish up my skills on Hebrew.'

'And who was that with?'

'You would not understand the man's name because it is not written anywhere.'

'He was a friend of the wise man?'

'He was well known to the wise man, yes.'

'So you would go there on a regular basis?'

'Yes, for two or three months at a time. It was a three-day journey, so I'd stay for two or three months and then return.'

'Go down the road to Damascus, turn right, or you could have gone on the water. Did you go by water?'

'We went overland.'

'And so where you went, were there other people being taught healing, or was just you?'

'This was a man who lived on his own in the mountains. People would go to him for healing and philosophy.'

'Were there other people like you, in your contemporary world that you heard of, miles away but were doing the similar things?'

'I hadn't heard of anybody by name. I will say that, but I had heard of a few others who were very similar to me. But as for names, I will apologise, I didn't know of any, but I'm sure there must have been a lot.'

'The question comes up, was there friendship between Romans and locals, or was it always a tense occupation situation?'

'Like all occupation situations, there was good and bad on both sides and some of the Romans were genuinely nice people.'

'And did they integrate with the population?'

'Some did, yes.'

'But obviously?'

'There was only a small handful.'

'And King Herod was a puppet for the Romans, yes? What was that about? Gain? Power?'

'Yes.'

'What about the story that he had all the first born baby boys killed in case they were you?'

'Wishful thinking, I think. He may have had it done within his main city, but how would they go out to every outlying village, every tribe that lived in the hills and do this? Even in your modern terms of today this would be physically impossible.'

'Hearing bush telegraph, people would hide their first born.'

'And what about the nomads? How would you cull those? You would have to find them first. A rather impossible task, I feel. It may have been something spoken about, but was never carried out.'

'I suppose it's a bit more of the shock-horror headline news.'

'Again, would you say the first born boy or the first born child?'

'First born boy.'

'In other words, he would have had to have massacred every man who was the first born as well.'

'There must have been an age limit.'

'Well, then, why couldn't one of them have been a man?'

'I think the story was the child that was born in the year of the census. But, I suppose a lot of them would have come after the census, like our friend.'

'Very misleading at times.'

'To go back to your birth, it was not recorded because you were born after your parents went to the census. So after the five or six years that you spent with the wise man, did you then go back to your parents?'

'No.'

'Where did you go?'

'I went travelling for a few years.'

'So you would have been 15/16. So where did you go travelling?'

'I will not be facetious and say round the world.'

'Thank you for that. Backpacking in Australia! These are what I presume are called your lost years?'

'I went to what you now call India and Pakistan and Persia.'

'And did some more learning and teaching?'

'There was not so much teaching, but learning and talking with wise men and the wise gurus of India.'

'They should be called the "found years" not the "lost".'

'Even to Tibet. I had five years of travelling.'

'So who accompanied you?'

'I was on my own. I picked up friends as guides and they would pass me on to other friends who were guides to help too.'

'So in the places that you went, was there an awareness that you were coming?'

'Why should there be?

'I don't know, I just assumed that they were all spiritually mediumistic and very wise. Were they aware of your—'

'Abilities?'

'Yes. So you spoke to, maybe, gurus or wise men in India or other countries?'

'On a similar wavelength, yes.'

'But they weren't expecting you. And you learnt a lot of different things from these people?'

'Yes, a lot of different things, a lot of different languages and lots and lots of knowledge.'

'In what sort of area? Healing, astrology, spiritual growth?'

'All of the tools of the trade. Basically, meditation and how to heal yourself. Trance, altered states of consciousness. Again if I had gone with ten or fifteen friends, I would have stuck out like a sore thumb.'

'Of course.'

'A man travelling on his own with two or three friends or two or three guides, they are very inconspicuous.'

'Did you get help with the languages? I'm looking at well over ten to get there. Were you a quick learner with language?'

'I was a quick learner, yes. I had, I will call them friends, even though they were guides, friends who spoke the local language and helped me through things. There were one or two things that I got stuck on, but I had learned enough to get me through.'

'You had been brought up multi-lingual. Did you not miss your family while you were having your travels?'

'At times.'

'Did your family know where you were?'

'There was always communication or letters between us.'

'How would letters get through?'

'First-class post! A letter would take two or three months to get there, but there were still people, coming back to friends and guides, who knew where we were or where we were going. One set of guides may have left you in one place. Knowing where you were headed they could advise other guides and sometimes get letters there ahead of you. We had quite an efficient postal system.'

'You touched on the Silk Road obviously?'

'Yes.'

'So there would have been communication both ways?'

'Yes.'

'Did you have experience of brigands and attacks en route?'

'We were lucky at times, but this is why we kept it to small numbers. Bigger numbers and we would have been an ideal target for them. Two or three people on their own they think, oh, a pile of beggars going to the next town.'

'But also presumably you had divine protection, did you?'

'I suppose so, yes. I think this was one of the skills I had been taught by one of the wise men – how to defend ourselves.'

'What we would consider now as martial arts?'

'Of course, yes.'

'You say you had travelled for five to six years and you were with the wise man five to six years as well, so after that you would have been around 21/22 and then what did you do?'

'I returned home. I felt I had had my adventure, but I had my family back at home and I wanted to see them.'

'And were they still living in the same place and when you got back did they recognise you?'

'Of course.'

'And were they well?'

'As you said, I had a brother and sister as well and, I wouldn't say they were grown up, but they were growing up.'

'Were they still there? There must have been a really joyous time, really pleased to see each other. Presumably you now had to decide what it was you wanted to do. You must have been aware now what the purpose was?'

'I knew what my purpose was. Maybe this is why I had to have a year gap.'

'Yes, a gap year. Because you knew how horrendous that was going to be?'

'No, but I knew my life would be taken up with other things.'

'Then suddenly you decided it was time you went public, as such. How much of that is as it is recorded in the books?'

'There is some truth in it. One of the first things that I do remember is the complete disrespect of the temple by the money lenders. That is one tale in the scriptures, in the Bible, and it is true. Again some of it may have been elongated, but I found that highly offensive.'

'You took a lot of risk to do that.'

'But even the elders were there standing back and, as you say in your modern terms, taking backhanders from them.'

'Was there at least one elder who was pure of intent, as such, and he was the one you found most affinity with?'

'Yes, I suppose the eldest one. It may be ridiculous, but he was, I should say, pure of heart.'

'And you kept up a friendship with him until he passed?'

'Yes, and again the rest of the stories are that I did get around. Talking to people as I think I have said to you in the past, I was quite radical in the way I spoke and what I spoke about. I always spoke from my heart.'

'This speaking, did you do it in the synagogues, or anywhere?'

'Open fields, anywhere where people would quietly gather...'

'Did people follow you because they saw you had a message? There must have been some that just were camp followers and wanted to join in this thing. You obviously knew which was which?'

'Yes.'

'You were considered a free thinker, a radical person who wanted to change how the establishment was at the time, and, I suppose you even get that in this day and age. You get people who are very persuasive and can ensnare people into a certain way, but it seems to me that it was much more than that that you were doing. You were getting people to think for themselves as well. It wasn't, "you'll live to a good old age if you think this", there were no promises made with it, it was just seeing things as they were. I'm rabbiting a bit, I know, but are you making sense of what I am saying?'

'Oh, yes.'

'Tell me where I have gone wrong, then.'

'You were doing all right.'

'Right, because obviously, you know, we want to reflect your thoughts and your memories in this book.'

'Again, I did not preach from the scriptures.'

'No.'

'I did not impose my thoughts on anyone. And like you would say in your modern times, I was trying to get them to expand their minds. As your friend Merlin says, thinking out of the box. Be truthful to yourselves.'

'How successful do you feel you were about freeing up people's minds because there is a category of people when presented with a new idea, they take the whole lock, stock and barrel as gospel rather than seeing it as a key to expand the mind? Do you feel you had success there, because it might be very difficult with channelled religion with so much ritual?'

'I felt I did succeed with many and maybe this is why I was so popular in other ways. You know we were a country occupied by the Romans, so to have someone like myself spouting forth words of wisdom was quite dangerous for me and even for those who wished to follow.'

'Were you often, in our parlance, pulled in by the authorities for sedition, with someone taking you aside saying, "Hey, you are going too far"?'

'Not so much with the authorities, it was with the religious elders, who supposed I was taking their control away. They had control of the masses and I was unlocking the gates for the masses, which they did not like.'

'Did the Romans feel you were raising people up against their rule?'

'One or two did, but I feel a lot of the higher authority was, I don't mean to say dismissive of me, but, "he is not doing us any harm, he is keeping the people happy, so just let him be".'

'So it was more the elders?'

'It was more the religious establishment that was against me rather than the Romans themselves.'

'Nothing new there really, is there? It was quite a good thing for the Romans to have a division, in the divide-and-rule thing – talking amongst themselves rather than against the occupiers.'

'I suppose, in a way, I was quite a diversion for them, in a positive way.'

'It is interesting, isn't it, because there are similarities to modern-day times? But you don't think of it in that way really. It seems that because they dressed so differently, lived so differently, you think of things being so different, but there are so many similarities there. But you did say that it was very much like our modern life at the moment – the head, the thinking stuff – did you not?'

'Yes. There has been much changed in your modern, material world compared with what we had then, but the authoritarian side of things has changed very little at all.'

'When you were doing your – going around and talking – what sort of area was that in?'

'All around the area where I was born, all around… Oh, dear me, what you would call the Holy Land now.'

'And, as you went, was it then that you performed these so-called miracles?'

'It was supposedly, yes.'

'I mean there are numerous miracles that were mentioned, curing the blind man and the leper. And how accurate are these?'

'Some are accurate, some are wishful thinking. And with the leper, there were ten.'

'Ten lepers?'

'Nine out of the ten did not return to me, only one did. That was done with herbs over a period of weeks, not a day. They had leprosy coming on, they did not have it full blown, so herbs, other things and, of course, healing.'

'And with the blind man?'

'Herbs again.'

'Right. Over a period of time?'

'He had what you would call a detached retina, and herbs and rest were enough over three or four weeks and, of course, healing this brought his sight back.'

'And so, with time, these acts of yours became a demonstration of miracles?'

'Yes.'

'And even, I mean, you have already spoken before about the feeding of the 5,000. It wasn't 5,000, and the loaves were this big,' demonstrates. 'The loaves were quite big and the people may have been 100 or so.'

'As you would say today, they had a little snack or sandwich just to fill in the gap, which again, would tide them over until they returned to their homes for a proper meal.'

'Smorgasbord. What about one of the stories when you were on the boat in the Sea of Galilee, and the fishing had dried up and apparently you said—?'

'Cast the net down the other side.'

'That's right. And was that true again?'

'When you have, I will not say been a fisherman, but if you have been on the water and you look, you can see the discolouration of the water when the fish are drawing near and sometimes, as we all know, we all get into despair. So there's more luck than judgement, cast on that side.'

'That is what is recorded as a success story. Did you have any times that didn't actually produce results?'

'Quite often – times when we spent many hours completely fishless. And another one, before you ask, about calming the waters. I was sleeping on the boat and a storm had blown up. And if people were to know, the Sea of Galilee is renowned for storms blowing up out of nothing and settling down from nothing. As it was, a storm had blown up and they were all panicking and I told them, "Don't worry, the storm will be finished soon", and within a few moments the storm had blown itself out. Another story binned.'

'What about your appearance? Were you like the image that is portrayed today?'

'Which part – long hair and a beard? Sandals, yes, because sandals were the dress of the day. Long hair and beard, well, there was no time to have a haircut or a shave, so, easy to wear isn't it?'

'Interesting that you are always portrayed as fair, which in that part of the world would be surprising. Betrayed by the fair hair. So what colour was your hair?'

'What colour do you think I would have had?'

'Black.'

'Black, yes.'

'You were always given golden hair to match the halo.'

'What colour do you think my beard was?'

'Black, blackish grey? Reddish?'

'Black with, I do not say sticks of red, but tinges of red or ginger.'

'Who was your hairdresser? You would have worn headgear, would you not?'

'Yes, just a...ruff.'

'But not like the modern Arabs?'

'No, just like a... I was going to say a tea towel, but I can't think of the right word or phrase to use. But it was like light scarf to keep the sun from giving you sunstroke. And again, not so much white robes but just comfortable robes, to keep you cool in the heat of the day.'

'So, from your going around, doing your talking, did this now last from the age of about the early 20s right up until the crucifixion?'

'Yes.'

'And when did you meet Mary? How old were you when you met Mary?'

'I met Mary on, if you could call it that, my tour.'

'So she wasn't from your community? Where was she from?'

'I cannot remember where that was now, but she was another free spirit, was wandering, I suppose.'

'All on her own?'

'With three or four friends.'

'And joined your entourage?'

'Yes, she was from a well-to-do family, who had, I do not know the right words to use for your modern terms.'

'Was she ethnically different to you?'

'I feel she was more from the north, when I was from the middle to south.'

'Of?'

'My village, of Nazareth.'

'Oh, so she was from the same country?'

'Yes. I suppose in a way maybe she was of royal blood, which would be your modern term to use, but again she was a free spirit like myself.'

'How old were you when you met her?'

'Twenty-five, twenty-six.'

'And how old was Mary when you met her?'

'Twenty-one, twenty-two.'

'And she had experience in healing and knowledge of herbs?'

'She was from a different financial class than I was, if you want to put it in that term, which then for the better-off families was a part of the education for a young woman.'

'Dealing with knowledge of herbs?

'Yes.'

'And meditation? She must have been quite defiant and feisty?'

'Yes.'

'Obviously she had not married early and had lots of children, as they were wont.'

'Again she was not a disappointment to her father, her mother maybe, but her father, I felt he knew his daughter would fly the nest and do her own thing, and I felt she left with his backing, or with his blessing, I should say.'

'Blessing! He must have been a very unusual and very wise man. There is something I am a bit confused about – I'm sure everyone else understands it, but do I understand that you lived in Bethlehem, or just outside, whilst the census was on and then went and grew up in Nazareth, so your family stayed in Bethlehem for a year or so?'

'A few months. Again the census then was not like it is today, filling in a piece of paper and then returning it. It would have been an actual head count.'

'A spot check, they would have to see you. And was this for the Romans? It sounds like a Roman kind of job. So probably they were quite bureaucratic. Definite about what you had to do. And that brings up other questions – it must have changed society so much when the Romans came in because I presume they were quite laid back and lived quite simple lives and then the Romans come in and impose their—'

'Totalitarian society.'

'How long had the Romans been in power?'

'Too long.'

'Before you arrived – 100 years?'

'I cannot remember I do not know at the moment.'

Chapter Two

Spreading the Word

'So, asking about Mary and your courtship.'

'But what is there to know?'

'Tell us how you progressed with getting to know her.'

'She just joined me as a free spirit, which she was.'

'What about parental approval on both sides? Did your parents and hers approve of the liaison, as such?'

'They didn't really know at the time, as I have said, she was a feisty free spirit, she rebelled against what she was and what she was expected to do, she didn't want to be a handmaiden to anybody.'

'What did her family expect her to do?'

'She was, as I have said, born into what you would call royalty, so she was expected to go down the royal road and marry whoever was thrown at her, but being the lady that she was, this wasn't for her. As I said, she studied healing and other things, and herbs, which was a little bit out of order for a young woman of that time, especially with royal blood in her!'

'What royalty was she was born to? Who were her parents?'

'This I cannot remember at the moment, I will be very honest with you.'

'Did you meet them?'

'No.'

'And was there a reason or was it was just that you were too busy?'

'Too busy and they lived, I wouldn't say the other side of the world, but many more miles away than we could travel.'

'Tradition has it that you are descended from the line of David – was that her line?'

'Yes, my apologies for not remembering. But if they had known what she was doing and getting involved, in your modern terms, with a down-and-out as myself, this would have severely gone against the grain.'

'I am interested in why you say a "down-and-out" because you had had an education.'

'But I was a "nobody" compared with royalty. The same as your modern days, how often do royalty marry out of the family?'

'I am sorry to hark back to this David thing but in the holy book it says that you were born of David's line, but you weren't?'

'If I was to be born of David's line, would not my mother, Mary, have been in the royal family? Another small quirk that has been altered for the sake of keeping the masses under the thumb.'

'But even if you just look at the Bible as it is, it goes against the grain, because it says it traces your genealogy back to David and yet in the next breath it says you were born of the Holy Spirit. They can't have it both ways!'

'And, of course, the perfect virgin birth as well!'

'It's a little bit of a jump, but a question that in fact my son asked today and I was explaining that nobody had written anything down for so long, for 100 years, I think you said, and he said, "What about the disciples?" because there are the different disciples' books, aren't there? Matthew, Mark Luke and John. Did not they record events at the time?'

'They saw the events, but again they were not written until many years later.'

'And presumably they weren't always around at every event?'

'Yes, of course.'

'So they wrote it from another perspective, and my guess is that they weren't natural writers.'

'No disrespect to the people we have sitting here, but it is like keeping your own personal diary – you write the way you speak sometimes, rather than the proper written words, use abbreviations and codes.'

'But even so, in your time would they have kept diaries, or would they have kept records at all?'

'No records, just what was remembered.'

'So when it was finally written down it was from word of mouth?'

'Of course. It was translators and you know how things go missing in translation.'

'And probably through a generation of hearsay, wasn't it?'

'The knowledge would have been passed on nearing death. The information would have been passed on, I'm not saying literally on your deathbed, but important events would be filled into the memory bank to be passed on.'

'And embellished?'

'Of course, we have to make a decent story of something, don't we?'

'And so with every year that passed, the fantasy of it became bigger and bigger, and because you were revered by these people, you became a lot more infallible, as such.'

'And a question to ask you and to ask your own personal church leaders, if I am so revered, and held in such high esteem, why did they want me dead?'

'Because you were a threat to their authority.'

'Of course, but if I was such, in modern-day terms, a rebellious terrorist as I was seen by some, why am I so celebrated thousands of years later? Are they too pigheaded to admit their faults, or is it sheer guilt that made them put me on a pedestal. Maybe something to ask your, I was going to say, church leaders, but if you ever have the opportunity, it is something to ask them.'

'It is something that I have thought a lot about and particularly at the moment, but I happen to be singing Bach's *St Matthew Passion*, which is from Matthew's book, and your presence, your life, inspired this most beautiful music and these most heartfelt apologetic words and there is such pain and even in singing it I think we all feel quite ashamed. Even in learning the words.'

'Why should you feel ashamed?'

'Because of what we did, because we are part of humanity and this is what humanity did all those years ago.'

'But it wasn't humanity.'

'Wasn't it?'

'Were you to blame for my so-called crucifixion?'

'Well, I feel partly to blame because I'm part of humanity, I suppose.'

'But did you have a hand in my crucifixion?'

'No, I don't think so.'

'Then why do you feel guilty for the sins of others?'

'Right.'

'If a man goes and robs a shop, takes all their money, do you feel guilty for what he has done?'

'No, I suppose not.'

'Well, you should do the way you are talking now.'

'It just makes me very sad, and that's a different thing. Maybe this is what the Church wants to do.'

'Of course. Total control again, my friend.'

'Total control – your myth has become a sort of distraction from the real thing. They focus on what they have built up to control them and the guilt is very convenient, it keeps people in line, does it not?'

'It does. Again, just to put one final cap on it for you, the troubles you have in Afghanistan with the troops from many parts of the world that are being killed, do you feel guilty for them?'

'No.'

'Well, you should do again because they are a part of humanity.'

'I feel very sad for them.'

'It is sad, but you must not take on the guilt of others.'

'Right.'

'Because that is what is being preached from the pulpits to you. Do they who preach take the guilt on their shoulders? No, they slope it on to others who will take the guilt, because they do not have the courage to stand up and admit their guilt and apologise.'

'Is it true that at the time of your crucifixion there wasn't this whole religious thing, you were regarded as an upstart full stop and all the guilt stuff came a lot later when you were harnessed onto this religion?'

'Again, in a way you could say that this was my way of having my own religion, even though it was not. It was just my way of gathering people and talking, and occasionally going into trance, channelling words of wisdom from past masters who had walked the earth many years before I had.'

'Wonderful. Could you give us some idea of those past masters that you channelled, for instance?'

'Jacob...there were many. At the time I did not realise who they were but I just knew these were words to be shared with others.'

'So if other people, the rest of the world, followed your example as in your religion, as you put it, it would be a very different world today?'

'Again, from what I have seen there are many in the spirit realms who would agree, what has been the biggest cause of many wars and battles?'

'Religion. 'When you were in trance, gave these words out, the scriptures say nothing about hecklers. You must have had hecklers in every crowd that you addressed?'

'There always was.'

'How did you deal with them?'

'I completely ignored them. As you know, by ignoring them, they do not have the strength or the weapon to rebel. When you get a naughty child throwing a tantrum, if you pander to that tantrum, it will do it even more, yet if you tell them to stop and walk away and ignore them, what does that child do?'

'Gets tired and stops. So the problem with the authorities at that time is that they didn't ignore you?'

'No, some of the hecklers were sent by the authorities, of course. That is something that hasn't changed.'

'But they did take you as a serious threat?'

'Yes.'

'But they couldn't shut you up?'

'I suppose, in that way, I was seen as a serious threat. I have heard many times, that I was preaching or, preaching is not the right word because I do not like it, I was passing on the word and, as you would call it, the love of God, and the authorities did not like this, because, as far as they were concerned, there were priests and all the other silly religious paraphernalia they called themselves and they thought and believed they were only ones who could speak to God. You being a commoner cannot, because, one – you are not in a church or a synagogue, and two – you are not a priest so cannot have the right to speak to God.'

'When you talk of the authorities, you don't mean the Romans, you mean the elders?'

'The elders of the churches.'

'So they were the real stumbling block?'

'Pontius Pilate was a quite a quiet man, irrespective of what many things have been said about him.'

'How did the Romans see it? Did they see you as a threat or were they happy that you were actually dividing?'

'They were quite happy and contented. They saw me as somebody trying to settle the masses so they were happy with what was going on.'

'But also, with the religious structure there, you creating dissent would be favourably looked upon by the Romans because it would keep the interests bubbling. Divide and rule.'

'But again I had had many meetings with Pontius Pilate as well, private meetings and maybe like an audience with him like you now. He was what I would call a very humble man.'

'What was discussed then?'

'A general talk, it wasn't about what I was doing or what he was doing, it was as you would say, friends over a cup of tea, even though we were not friends in that way, but that is the easiest way that I can explain it.'

'It seems extraordinary to me that you would meet in each other's social circle.'

'And why not? He had his job to do and he was doing his job to the best of his abilities.'

'Sizing up the opposition.'

'But again, coming to the crucifixion side of things, I know we are jumping ahead a little bit, but who made the choices, myself or Barabbas? Again, coming back to our friend the hecklers or the authorities.'

'Did you speak to Barabbas? I'm sorry, we are jumping ahead. Did you have words with him when you were all under the authorities?'

'I just told him to be himself and be a man, and again there is nothing that has come out about him, but he changed his ways from a robber to somebody quite gentle.'

'Did you have friends in the Sanhedrin and the temple authorities and stuff like that? Did you have people who actually heard what you were saying?'

'I had no friends in there, no. As I have said in the past, I was upset and offended that they had money lenders in the churches and to call it the house of God was hypocritical. So there I had no friends. I know one or two did come along to look very plain in the crowd but you could always spot them.'

'What by their servants?'

'As my friend here will say, when you do your mediumship you can always spot the sceptics. It is exactly the same. It is something that you know within yourself.'

'Is it possible we could talk about the apostles and stuff like that? Who were they, were they your personal friends, or did you pick them up en route, i.e. people who heard what you were saying? Or were there other reasons why they were with you?'

''They were just as you said, stragglers that I picked up on the way. They were people who came to believe in what I was saying and what I was doing. And like myself, they wanted to change the world and the things around them.'

'Did those followers actually then move around with you and become a big group?'

'People joined and left.'

So, in fact, we were led to believe that there were 12 disciples, but I know from what you have said in the past that there were a lot more. What number roughly are we talking about?'

'There were about 25 to 30 who were what I would call really close, the rest were coming and going and in and out.'

'And of that 25 or 30, how many of them were women?'

'How many would you like to believe?'

'There were none? I bet there were half.'

'There were quite a few women who braved the religious authorities.'

'And did they bring their children with them?'

'Some of them came with children, yes. They had decided that this was what they wanted and their children came as well. Again it was a pleasure to have youngsters around rather than all the older ones, as I would call them, and they were from all walks of life and from all ages. They were not just as you would call in your modern-day terms "teenagers", or going back to what I'm sure some of you remember what they called the '60s.'

'Mods and rockers?'

'So, they were not all a bunch of young hippies, there were some old hippies, but we had a wide span of people following, they were not all youngsters.'

'To have these people following you could, at times, have been too much for you. Did you have any other interests or how did you grab a bit of time to yourself?'

'I quite often used to wander off for three or four days on my own, just for the solace and my own sanity, I suppose. I needed the break from the crowds.'

'Did you have any, what we would call hobbies or other interests? This fascinates me because I can't imagine you were on the case 100% of the time, because everyone needs a little light relief.'

'I used to carve little things from wood and make small toys for some of the children, so that was my relaxation and pleasure.'

'When you went off on your two or three days' solace, did you take Mary with you sometimes?'

'Yes.'

'So that you could have time together?'

'Special time for us as well.'

'How long was this period when you were travelling and with Mary?'

'Six, maybe seven years.'

'Did you ever go back to the same place?'

'We just wandered around from town to village. There was no set route, we just wandered aimlessly. But then as the word went round and spread, there were people saying, "would you come to our village" or "would you come to our town?" exactly as in modern-day terms now. "We would love to see you. We will feed and water you and we will look after you". And, of course, there were many artisans who had come with us as well, and they had so many skills that again, I suppose you could say there was trading going on. We did things for them and they provided us with food, so there was never anything, I wouldn't say we wanted, but we never expected anybody to give us something for nothing. We expected to work our way through, pay for our passage, if that is the right term. Helping in the fields sometimes, gathering the harvest, even helping to sow things.'

'Were you ever approached by royalty or those in higher positions to come to their town or their place of abode?'

'No.'

'Were there ever any towns that did not welcome you because of you and their religious beliefs?'

'There were one or two.'

'And also, the fact that there were 20 or over 25 of you must have been formidable for a small town or village?'

'Yes, for a small village having all of us to descend on them. Some of them were frightened of the authorities, and not the Roman authorities, that was, but the religious authorities.'

'And so would you just move on in those cases?'

'I would go in and see them myself, or Mary would come with me. I would talk to them privately and then go on our way, just to give them some reassurance that we understood why we were not welcome.'

'You didn't want to rock the boat?'

'Because we could have caused ructions for them and many of the villagers could have been killed for associating with us. So that was a sad fact in one way, but something we respected in others.'

'Did this happen from the beginning then, from the moment you started teaching?'

'Just after the word got out, yes.'

'So there was that threat all those years, which presumably got bigger and bigger and grew until the moment you came back to Jerusalem?'

'Why should I have been a threat, to lose their stranglehold which for over 2,000 years has not changed one small piece?'

'No, I meant that threat to you from the elders that grew, so it hasn't changed?'

'They talk in modern terms of this man Hitler who presided over World War II, but wasn't what the religions authorities did when I walked the earth a lot worse? They still have not learned the lesson or taken any knowledge from it, bar, as I have said, murdering me and then putting me on a great pedestal to worship me. To me, who is the biggest hypocrite, Hitler or the Church authorities? I will leave you to ponder that one.'

'Did you ever attend services in the synagogues and temples?'

'In my younger days, but later days, no.'

'Was that looked upon as sacrilegious by other people?'

'By the elders, yes.'

'Also by your contemporaries? Didn't you say by the age of 12 you were questioning the elders?'

'Between the age of six and twelve, yes.'

'So that started quite early, really?'

'Well, even in your modern-day terms, how many of your religious leaders take questioning. Has anybody ever questioned one?'

'Not out in the open.'

'Why? Because of who they are and it is not the done thing. But who told you it's not the done thing?'

'They did.'

'So again, what gives them the authority to be right all the time?'

'They did.'

'So what does it make them?'

'Hypocrites.'

'Yes. I am not wishing to start a revolution, but is it time that maybe modern man did verbally question the religious authorities?'

'The hierarchy of the Church?'

'All of them, I do not mean one little section, I mean the wider section across the world.'

'Well, so many people nowadays are voting with their feet, are they not? As we do here? We don't attend organised religious services because we have our own way of doing things.'

'And those religious leaders, I presume, are sitting on their backsides scratching their heads wondering why the place is empty. I am sure I could give you a few answers. One – it is cold. Two – who would like to sit on their backside on a hard wooden seat for an hour? Three – who wants a hypocrite preaching to them? Four – if it is supposedly a house of God, why is it adorned with so much gold and why does the vicar or the priest have to have gold garments on? Is this what my supposed father would have wanted? It just needs to be the way that I preached, simple. So, again, they are hypocrites to themselves.'

'I have a friend who is fighting for the ending of celibacy for Catholic priests, because it is all based on the assumption that you were celibate. Now this argument is quite strong because of all the wrongdoing in the Catholic Church that has happened.'

'But to me, I am not meaning to sound judgemental to any religion, but how can a Roman Catholic priest or a religious priest who has never ever been married give counselling to somebody who is married and who may be going through difficult times?'

'Oh, God will provide!'

'Hypocritical. But again, as I have said, I think in the past, or I have spoken to this one I know, why should God be blamed for everything, why should he have to sort all your problems out?'

'It's we who provide the ignorance here.'

'But why should God be blamed? Why would he want to sort your marriage out? He may want to say, I'm not getting involved in that lot, thank you, you sort yourselves out. I feel that is a very narrow-minded view to say that God will sort things out.'

'I suppose that is another way of controlling society, another way of giving lessons on how to behave.'

'When they cannot behave themselves.'

'But then like everything, we shouldn't tar them all with the same brush because there are many decent priests who believe in what they are doing and don't see it as a control. They actually believe they are doing God's work, because that's how they have been taught. They are good souls, just misled.'

'Misled by who? The higher authority that they are answerable to?'

'Yes, I would want to say that too, because I've met some remarkable priests.'

'But they still won't be drawn in certain areas, they still have the dogma around them, so they are still, no matter how good, self-limiting, aren't they?'

'So, it all boils down to control again. That is something that I never had over people. I could have done, but I didn't. They chose to come and listen and walk with me sometimes. If they didn't, well, I wasn't going to get broken-hearted and force them into slavery with me, if you put it that way.'

'But then with this book, it's obviously not going to go down very well with the churches, because it's going to make people maybe think about what is going on, which is obviously the idea of it.'

'Well, you know when the words come out, what are you going to be called?'

'Probably something similar to what you were called – heretics.'

'Antichrists – the Devil has risen!'

'How dare they presume to talk to JC – to Jesus? They wouldn't call you JC would they? Sorry.'

'What makes them more special than you or anyone else? As I have said many times, and it is even written in the Bible, you are all God's children, he loves you all, so why would he decide to send St Peter to the Pearly Gates to say you have been bad, you cannot come in, you've got go down to Hell. What a load of rubbish! And according to the scriptures, is not God all loving and all forgiving? So, why have you got to answer to things, mistakes that you made on the earth? To me, my views on that are that all the religious bigots who are in the background pulling the strings, if there is such a place as Hell then that is where they will all go, not through the Pearly Gates where they think they will go. I know it does not work that way, but that is a penny for my thoughts.'

'But I mean people have got free will, so whatever they jump up and down and say, they are losing the control that they have had, because more people want to think for themselves.'

'Well, how many? Look in this country of England, how many people are turning from, I will call them mainstream religions, back to, I know what this one calls the old ways, going back to the grass roots before the religions became religions, back to the Pagan sides and the Shaman sides? Back to, I'm not saying to worship Mother Nature, but for that road? Again, like yourselves, the spiritual road and the spiritual pathway. Forget about the religious side of the spiritual, but the true spiritual pathway. A lot more maybe than people would think or want to admit to.'

'Can we go back to your life?'

'Yes, I am sorry.'

'No, it is very interesting, thank you. We were talking about you on the road to the different villages etc. When you visited these villages, how long would you stay and what sort of things would you talk about to them for such a long time?'

'Sometimes it would be a day or two days, sometimes two or three weeks. Again on the work side, it would depend on the season. If we had come into the village and the summer was in and the harvest was being gathered and they were short of help, then we would stay a bit longer to help them get the crops in. Because again, we were being paid or fed and watered, so it was a "give and take" from both sides. And sometimes we would only stay a day because we needed fresh water and things and it may have been a small village with ten or a dozen houses. But wherever we went, as I have said, we always had a very warm welcome. Again there were always the few that were cold, but it is still down to modern society. Just the same now, is it not? And what would we talk about? We would talk about some of my life and exchange ideas and things and, as you would say, have open discussions. We would do your modern-day clairvoyance, bringing loved ones from spirit through for them.'

'And healing?'

'Yes, healing, and occasionally we would have an open-air service, again at which either myself or Mary would go into trance and, as I have said, channel words from the masters or people of great knowledge.'

'Both you and Mary did that? Fascinating.'

'I was, I do not mean to sound big headed, I was the main one and Mary would chip in on that. But again, on the other hand, Mary was a more evidential medium than I was, so we both had our balance of skills. But I know that it was something that was not done very often or in the open, and I know from yourselves with what you do now, how much pleasure you can get with being reunited with one who has passed. So that is something that has been forgotten.'

'I see no mention of it at all.'

'Why does this not surprise me?'

'Were there any other people like you working in the same area?'

'There were quite a few similar, yes.'

'Were they recognised?'

'It was all very much how your modern spiritualism was, it had to be kept very quiet for fear of repercussions and breaking the law, but it was the law of the religions and the elders rather than the law of the land.'

'It seems funny that it was such a religion of seers and prophets all along the line, and yet they didn't recognise the lesser.'

'The common man was not allowed.'

'So, seers were allowed if you were a registered elder or something like that?'

'But again if you went to Greece, I wouldn't say they were common, but it was very normal to come across them, they were accepted, and it was accepted that people could have foresight and see and hear from the spirit realms. But to come to the other side of the Mediterranean, to my birthplace, the religious leaders had a stranglehold.'

'The Greeks have always been much freer, haven't they? And they had such a history in ancient Greece, I suppose it gave them a different way of being. In modern-day spiritualism, some of the finest mediums have been barely able to read or write, and yet they have been wonderful mediums for bringing trance and messages and the rest of it, so at least that seems to be a step forward in this day and age.'

'Again, to prove the authorities wrong, why do you always have to be highly educated to achieve anything? I was not highly educated, but I was lucky enough to have friends who knew people who took me under their wing and allowed me to learn.'

'So, as such you were highly educated, you were specifically educated in relevant topics, do you see what I mean? When you are talking about education, some of it is relevant and some isn't.'

'Usually with education, you talk of academia rather than healing and spiritual knowledge and that seems to be something that nowadays is completely lost. A lot of the learning that our children do now is so irrelevant and yet, the learning that you did was so pertinent to what you needed to know.'

'As I have heard said for your modern times with your modern children, they are only being taught to pass exams, they are not being taught knowledge. And then they wonder why the modern youth is lost, even in their early to mid 20s.'

'So, those things that you talked about learning before were languages, astrology, herbs and healing. Those were the main ones?'

'And philosophy. You cannot go to Greece without studying or reading philosophy.'

'The wisdom of past masters again.'

'All right, some of them may be heavy going or beyond you, but like everything, you can take one small segment for yourself.'

'Take from it what you can. All of those things together helped you understand people and be able to communicate with people and also to understand the environment, the cosmos and the healing environment. They were just all the most important things, weren't they? What a lesson we could learn from that!'

'Even with the healing and, I know some of you do this as well, but have you ever thought that astrology may be able to help you with healing at times?'

'I'd like to understand that more. I've thought it, but I don't know it.'

'Or even the phases of the moon. Experiment with yourselves, those of you who are healers, see which times you are weak and which times you are strong and if you can find your balance, think, "Well, the day before the full moon the healing was mediocre, but two days after the full moon my healing was powerful". So make all your appointments for two or three days after, to get the maximum strength for what you are doing.'

'That's interesting. I have seen someone recently doing a similar thing with gardening. This is a good time for plants and a good time for sowing and at certain times of the day even, quite specific times of the day, but I hadn't thought of it in terms of healing. My sister bakes her bread according to the times of the month. She will say, "I had to bake bread today. I didn't want to because the signs aren't right and it wasn't nearly as good as it should have been".'

'And this does work. Again, old ways that sometimes have been forgotten.'

'That is such a wonderful thought, especially the healing.'

'Even look to the alignment of the stars and the planets. A simple experiment for you. You do not need a telescope to be an astrologer.'

'So, where would we start from this place where I know very little?'

'From the beginning!'

'Thank you.'

'Start with the moon. Look at what is simple. Look at the moon phase tonight. When do you next have healing?'

'Wednesday.'

'Look at the moon Tuesday night and then Wednesday do your healing and see how you felt, maybe even make a note of it, then when you have your next healing session, look at the moon again and see how you felt and what was coming for you, and if you feel one was better than the other, then this is just a simple start, there's nothing difficult. Forget about all your text books.'

'Thank you. That's a very good thought, I'll do that. I have just acquired a spiritual calendar that talked about the phases of the moon and I knew it was really significant and now I know why.'

'How do you think the modern and the old shaman works?'

'From the same position.'

'The weather, the phases of the moon, the sun, whatever the day is like, the clouds, they didn't just study them for the sake of looking up to the sky, there were very relevant reasons. Again, life is so simple but modern man has made it so difficult.'

'That wonderful combination again, that things that are spiritual are simple and very profound, so they are both accessible and yet amazing. Thank you, that's a really good thought.'

'Sorry if I have gone off track a bit, my friends. Now you understand why I studied astrology.'

'I wish I had that knowledge now.'

'You have, as and when you wish to tap in.'

'It's all inside, isn't it?'

'Of course. Then again, is it relevant for your life at the moment? If it is not, it will stay in the memory bank until you are ready.'

'I'm going to find that really helpful.'

'Good.'

'Okay. So carrying on again, you've just told us what you talked about and how many days you stayed with people. Now, just going back to Mary Magdalene, did you marry Mary Magdalene, and can you tell us when and where?'

'Well, one, it was not as you would say, a proper wedding ceremony as you would know them nowadays. We couldn't marry in a church.'

'It was a civil ceremony?'

'That is a good way of putting it, my friend, we just made our vows and that was it.'

'So were you legally married at that time?'

'In the Church's eyes, no.'

'In the eyes of the law were you?'

'No.'

'But in your eyes you were?'

'And in the eyes of what you call God.'

'And where did this civil ceremony take place?'

'In the middle of nowhere!'

'And was anyone else there?'

'A few friends. Really close friends.'

'Would any of those be names that we know? Could you tell us, please?'

'Yes, my best friend, Judas.'

'Right, that's going to blow up the Church, isn't it? And who else?'

'My friend, the wise man and his lady wife.'

'Were there any family members?'

'No, just a word of blessing from Mary's father.'

'Really!'

'We did do the decent thing of informing him and he just wanted the best for his daughter, for her to be happy, and that was all he wanted from life.'

'He was a remarkable man.'

'He was, even though I never met him personally because again, after the crucifixion, we had to just disappear. It would not have been fair on my family or even Mary's family.'

'I wonder where Mary's family thought she had gone.'

'They knew she had gone to France.'

'But they didn't know why. When you married, how long was it before the crucifixion took place?'

'Two years.'

'And where did you marry? Apart from being in the middle of nowhere, was there a place name or a country name?'

'Brazil. Would that do you?'

'Do you not remember?'

'It would have been what you know as Judea. My apologies for my cheek!'

'Refreshing. And so can you tell us the events leading up to the crucifixion, because I feel we are moving towards that now, or have I missed out something?'

'How do you mean, missed out on something?'

'I am not jumping forward too much? Do I get the impression that, as you became better known, as the word spread about your teaching with Mary, that tension increased and so it was that it was moving towards an inevitable confrontation? And despite this, you deliberately went back to Jerusalem to fulfil "the prophesy"?'

'And what was "the prophesy"?'

'I don't know. I was going to ask you!'

'And how could I fulfil a prophesy that never was?'

'That was the question really. Did you know what would happen, or was it just that you expected that things would get more difficult?'

'We knew things would get more difficult but they got deeper than what I suppose even you yourselves would ever have imagined, even in your modern times. It is like this book we are putting together now, we know the difficult times are coming in but you are still forging ahead with it. It is exactly the same as me and my followers.'

'You knew you had to keep going?'

'Yes, it was one of those things, but I do feel quite angry at times, even though the Romans were invaders of our country, why should they have to take the blame all the time for what had happened to me? I know there were good and bad on all sides, as even you know in your modern times, there are good soldiers and bad.'

'Were the Romans doing what the local authorities wanted them to do as occupiers? Kind of "their duty"?'

'Yes keeping the big bosses sweet.'

'And Pilate washed his hands of the whole deal?'

'Yes, he basically had got fed up with being in Jerusalem and the whole affair. He wanted to go back home to Italy. I know he had his wife and children with him, but he was homesick and he wished to go back to Italy and settle down and retire from the army and have what you would call "a normal life".'

'There is a thing called Palm Sunday when you allegedly entered Jerusalem on a donkey. Why should that have been passed down through the ages as something significant? What was all that about?'

'It was when we returned to Jerusalem, yes, but again I suppose religious bigots had to have their own way.'

'Because in the official story, you were welcomed and everybody threw palm fronds down and blah, blah, blah. Your notoriety had obviously risen quite a lot and people wanted to see you as a spectacle, I suppose, and I can't imagine for one minute that all of them were on your side.'

'Definitely not!'

'And yet the Church makes out that you were hailed—'

'Welcomed with open arms. It was not the case. It was just lovely, general people, the people who may have had relatives in other villages or little towns that we had passed through or seen and spoken to and the word had just come forward like that.'

'How did you feel about being welcomed like that?'

'Embarrassed.'

'Did you feel it was inappropriate?'

'Not inappropriate, but the way things were, with the occupation and everything else, they had to have something to look forward to and something to bring a smile back to their faces again. So we took away the pain of the occupation and all the other bad things that were going on around them.'

'So the authorities used you as a sort of focussing point at that time?'

'It was a little like being given an apple, but with the apple in one hand and a big stick in the other hand to crack you round the ear as soon as you took the apple.'

'Did you feel you had to return to Jerusalem? Was there something compelling you?'

'I went back to see my parents on the outskirts of Jerusalem and just say hello and maybe cheerio to people.'

'Why would you be saying cheerio at that time? Did you know what was going to happen?'

'The great escape.'

'So the question is, what was planned? What did you know? I suppose—'

'Well, we did know the authorities were plotting against us, which they had done from day one, and they were getting more and more powerful and they were arresting rebellious Roman soldiers from their own armies, if you want to put it like that, rather like your modern-day mercenaries. The response by the Church was: if anything happens, we do not know what you have done. It is nothing to do with us, but we will pay your wages. Because the people were getting thoroughly fed up with the occupation and there was talk of uprising and turning against the Romans. What better scapegoat than myself and my humble followers?'

'So did you ride into Jerusalem having this escape already planned out?'

'Yes, we knew things would go wrong, but they may have gone further wrong than what we anticipated.'

'You didn't anticipate being crucified!'

'No.'

'So, can you take us through the steps of what happened leading up to your crucifixion, for instance, the last supper?'

'Now where shall I start?'

'At the beginning!' Laughter.

'I have dug myself into a hole here, have I not, my friend? Well, from coming into Jerusalem and being welcomed, all right the welcome may not have been as glorious as has been spoken about over many years, but there was still a welcome from the people who loved us and wanted to hear us speak. This got up the noses of the authorities. We were welcomed and fed and watered very well, but we knew there were spies in the midst who were trying to get close to us, and I do know that there was one or two who were supposed to be close and who were quite easily bribed. So, this was where the rock of the master plan fell apart.'

'I know Judas was your close friend, but was the betrayal bit transferred onto him from other people who were bribed?'

'Yes. He was, as we had discussed many days later, if things were to really go awry, he was to sell my soul, if you want to put it like that.'

'For what purpose?'

'To get money from the churches in order to give back to the poor, who they had stolen from in the first place. They thought that they were paying him off for me, but knowing we would survive, the money could be returned to the poor people to give them a little bit of a better life.'

'And was that money returned to the poor?'

'Some, but I will tell you more of that later, because we do not wish to jump the gun too far. But on the run-up to the crucifixion, again, this was all lies put together from the high priests because of their jealousy of what I could do and what I was doing. We had to go and live on the outskirts of Jerusalem for a while, and we had to sneak around in the dark and at night to make communication with others. Again, we knew that Pilate didn't really want to get involved. All he wanted, as I have said earlier, was to return home.'

'He wanted to go back to Rome. Was that the general feeling in the army?'

'He did, his wife and children had returned earlier, he was lonely and homesick and he was missing his family. Again, with coming up to the crucifixion, this happened a week or ten days before I was arrested and accused of blasphemy against the churches and you name it. They came up with the silly idea.'

'So how did the priests actually arrange that, because if Pontius Pilate did not want to get involved, how did they get him to cooperate?'

'They lied their back teeth off.'

'Until, in the end...?'

'It didn't go to Pontius Pilate, it went to one of the other ministers around him. Pilate was not told until many days later.'

'That you had been arrested? And so where were you taken then?'

'To one of the local dungeons and incarcerated there.'

'And were you questioned there?'

'No, just locked up.'

'And then? Please continue.'

'He did come and speak to me one evening, sending his apologies for what had happened because he did not know, and that he would do his utmost to get us free.'

'Who are "us"?'

'Or get me free and allow me and my followers safe passage from Jerusalem, so that is why I said "us".'

'Round about this point, a label comes up of "Jesus of Nazareth, King of the Jews". Where did that originate, because according to literature, you are accused of claiming to be that, and at the trial it was mentioned?'

'I will ask you a question back before I answer.'

'Go ahead.'

'To all of you, where do you think?'

'The elders?'

'As I said – trumped-up charges.'

'So it wasn't anything that you said that was misinterpreted about the kingdom?'

'No, it was their way of getting revenge, I suppose, the only way they could do it was, as I said earlier, to lie their back teeth out.'

'To gain the support of the populace?'

'Yes, but again with the pressure put on Pontius Pilate from the elders, he had no other option but to agree with them, to try to keep the peace at a time when there were threats of rebellion.'

'He wanted to go home.'

'Yes. So really, in a way, all he wanted was a peaceful life until he returned which, until this day, I cannot blame him for. I feel, if your friends here were in a very similar situation, you would do exactly the same as he did. I am not saying you would or you wouldn't, but it is a very difficult scenario.'

'So the elders warned the Roman authorities that a rebellion was afoot, which it probably wasn't.'

'Yes, and they could control it by getting rid of me, because I was the ringleader. So as my friend here was saying, if you were in Pontius Pilate's situation, what would you do?'

'A difficult one isn't it?

'Yes. Well, carry on then, I just want peace and quiet. I feel I would have done the same.'

'He would have had to appease the people and the elders.'

'So, in fact, he was just another pawn in the chess game. But I feel at times that he has been somebody who has been rather misrepresented.'

'And you don't attach any blame at all, or you don't hold any sort of malice against him?'

'I suppose in another way, maybe the way the elders had put it to him, was it either his life or mine? I am not saying it was that easy but again, was that the pressure that they put the man under?'

'And his job description really was to—'

'Keep the peace in Jerusalem.'

'So, at what stage did Judas do the dropping of information for money?'

'Two days before. He didn't come and see me every day because there were different ones we could trust, Mary and a few others. We knew there were going to be problems and we had to try and remaster the master plan.'

'Right, so you were expecting to be arrested when you were, and then how long were you in this dungeon for before things changed?'

'How do you mean, things changed?'

'Before they crucified you.'

'A week.'

'Can I just go back a little bit before that? I just wondered about the steps before you were arrested, when you obviously knew you were going to be arrested. So there were various scenarios that have been talked about quite a lot, like the garden of Gethsemane and the last supper and things like that. I just wondered about the truth of those.'

'The last supper, well, we would always all, or as many of us as could, eat together anyway. We were all very sociable, but I suppose in a way the last supper was for those who were close to me, because we knew my arrest was imminent and so we had to formulate another plan which would come together a little bit later.'

'So all of the followers knew it was about to happen, they were all in on it, even perhaps those that—?'

'Betrayed us. I know now it was a mistake to confide in too many. But it doesn't matter now, you cannot change the past.'

'So therefore, what actually happened in reality at the last supper was totally different from what has been written about. Where it appears that you were warning them and they were quite shocked, from what's been written, it wasn't as if you were all singing from the same song sheet, but that you were on your own and they were separate in what they were thinking. In the literature you gave a definite feeling of finality and there was goodbye in your voice, and the disciples, the apostles, appeared to be shocked and ignorant of your plans.'

'I'm sorry, I had misunderstood you, my friend. There was, I suppose, two last suppers, one was a gathering of all of them to say our goodbyes, because we knew – a little close community of four or five of us – we were moving on from the country and that was the easiest way to say our goodbyes to them, knowing they would still carry on doing what they wanted to do, maybe even the work that we had been doing. But the final last supper was for Mary, Judas, myself and two other friends, who have not been named. This is where the plan was formulated for Judas to sell my soul, or sell me to the Romans for the money to pass on to the poor and where I would walk in the garden of Gethsemane. The scriptures say that I was saying my last goodbyes and praying for my soul, but I was doing nothing of the sort, I was just walking, waiting to be arrested.'

'So you were in the garden, which was the plan?'

'That is where Judas would come and kiss me on the cheek and do his part for the money, for the ransom, if you would put it that way, but he was a part of the overall master plan.'

'And these two suppers, was it first and second sitting on the same day or was it different days?'

'One was in the morning, or lunchtime, as you would say in your modern terms, and the other one was that very evening, but that was for a small group of five or six of them.'

'You mentioned about two other people, are you able to name them?'

'Not at the moment. At a later date I will tell you more, because they were the two that helped us go one way and the other way.'

'I thought that was the wise man and his wife. It was, wasn't it?'

'You jumped the gun and jumped the story, you see.'

'I'm sorry. And the arrest was there?'

'In the garden, yes.'

'At that point did you know what your fate would be?'

'We just presumed that we would be let off because of the Easter break, as you call it now.'

'So you got a lot more than you actually bargained for!'

'Yes.'

'When you say the Easter break, was it the Passover?'

'When criminals were freed, so we thought we would be out on this one. But again it didn't happen and as I said, I was imprisoned. Other things passed over during that week, which Judas came to tell me about, and we then made other plans.'

'Were you already in criminal status then? Were you "wanted"?'

'The elders wanted to get rid of me, so we formulated another plan, which, if things had come to the worst, is what we had planned for now. We thought that one would be able to disappear over the blue horizon, but as you know, all well-made plans never come to fruition. So we had to call on plan C, of which there wasn't even one!

If it did come to the fact of crucifixion, death by crucifixion anyway, they would give me some drugs, which would make me hallucinate and then slow my heart rate down to nothing. And then, things went on from there. Judas actually got the money, but he was betrayed by somebody inside who stole the rest of it, left 13 pieces of silver on him, and hanged him.'

'Somebody else hanged him?'

'He did not take his life, which is the one misconception in the Bible that bitters me.'

'Yes, because you were very close to him.'

'To have a good friend murdered in my name was deplorable, and for those who decided 100 years later what to put and what not to put in the Bible about my life story, to say that he was a traitor, when he was murdered by some of their predecessors, makes, to me, an utter mockery of your modern religion.'

'So it was the priests that murdered Judas?'

'Well, they had it done.'

'So the circumstances were quite damning, really. It looked bad for Judas.'

'But why was he singled out? He had a minor criminal record, he was caught stealing in his younger and childhood, days, and that was a stigma that went with him for ever. So, of course, we will have the thief. He will do. We can't have pure people, and of course as you said, my friend, because he was our friend. How would you put it in your modern terms? A little bit of a jack-the-lad and scoundrel, but not a horrible scoundrel. He was always up to mischief maybe, is that a better word to use? He would never harm or hurt anybody, but there was always the little bit of devil within him, the twinkle in his eye and always, is it the right words to use, wheeling and dealing?'

'Not criminal at all?'

'Not to make a fast buck from anybody, but he had always got this ability to barter.'

'Something on the go all the time?'

'But a heart of gold.'

'What was written about you in the names of Matthew, Mark, Luke and John, am I right in assuming that they didn't actually write those words, but they might have dictated it or related it at a certain date, and were they adjusted to fit in with—?'

'To fit in with the whole of the story, yes.'

'The official one.'

'Yes, I like that.'

'And that was done many years after, as you said.'

'I am looking at time now, whether or not we can talk about the crucifixion or whether we should leave it until the next time.'

'Yes, I think it may be better if we leave it for another session for you.'

'Each time, I think we have covered so much more than I expected us to, really. That is the nice thing in having a small, closely knit group like you.'

'Well, this is the greatest story ever told.'

'Thank you again, and thank you all for listening. And again, if there is anything that you think of between now and the next time we properly meet, even if it is going back over some of the old trails, please, please ask.'

'Yes.'

'Because I cannot always remember until I have had the proverbial kick into the backside to wake me up again. My memory banks are like yours, I need to be reminded at times.'

'Well, it is rather a long time ago! There is just one thing that occurs to me: last time when you spoke about miracles – turning the water into wine at the wedding – how did that come about?'

'Sleight of hand.'

'Oh, really? I thought perhaps, you know, you sort of not exactly hypnotised the wedding guests...'

'Mesmerised them?'

'Yes, you did, and so they were drinking water?'

'Coloured water.'

'And they thought it was the best wine. Right, thank you.'

'As you know yourself, my friend, you can hypnotise anybody into believing anything.'

'Yes, and there weren't many people there, I don't suppose. That's fine, thank you.'

'There were a few things that had come about, where people had been cured and other little things like the blind man. I don't know whether you know about him?'

'Yes, indeed.'

'He had got cataracts, as you call them now, in the very early stages, and me with my healing and Mary with her herbal knowledge, we stopped them from getting worse, and they actually cleared up in a couple of months.'

'Yes, I have read that in the last transcript.'

'Yes, it was not all over in a matter of seconds.' He shows signs of distress for a few moments.

'Are you okay?'

'Even with the man who was told to pick up his bed and walk, how do you think that one was?'

'He believed that he could? It was over a few days, over a few weeks?'

'Any other suggestions?'

'The lady with the issue of blood, who touched the hem of your garment and straightway she was healed.'

'Belief, sheer belief, but the man getting off his bed and walking, none of you have come up with the answer.'

'He'd never tried before?'

'He was just a lazy malingerer and he needed somebody to publicly humiliate him. Humiliate may not be the right word – but to give him the faith – you can get off your backside, you can walk. And he did, so it wasn't such a miracle after all, was it? Well, it was in a way, I suppose, because it gave him his faith back within himself.'

'Yes, he could go out and say, I have been healed, so now I can do this, that and the other.'

'I will leave you with that now, my friends. Thank you all very much for your precious time. Again, take my blessings, and to our friend here, work with the moon and see how it works. All of you, I am sure, but I know our friend here is more excited to try.'

Chapter Three

The Crucifixion

'Have you been in this situation before where you have been interviewed by people?'

'Everything that has been written has been hearsay and word of mouth. Those that remember and those that elongated a story, I suppose. This is the truth for once rather than the truth as other people have seen it, or wanted others to see it.'

'I am reminded of a text that was written about you and your hidden years, that you went as far as India. That text, where did it come from? Could it have been from you? Or was it hearsay?'

'Some was hearsay and maybe some from those who guided me and who travelled with me for a few days or weeks. As I have said, I did not have a constant companion and travelled on my own, although I did have other travellers with me at times for a certain distance.'

'Were you aware of chroniclers of your movements as it happened? Were there, what we call "diarists", who recorded a logbook of your travels, or were they all written a long time after the event?'

'A long time after the event. As I was travelling to India and around in India, nobody knew who I was. I don't wish to sound bigheaded, but I wasn't famous then, I was a "nobody", travelling and learning, like many others.'

'Yes, of course, because that was a seat of wisdom in North India. Did being there alter your outlook?'

'Not in the least. It gave me much more spiritual knowledge and a better insight into the world as a whole.'

'So that came after Greece and Turkey?'

'Yes.'

'They were in the latter years of your travelling, which I think you said were about six years?'

'Yes, but very, very enjoyable times. They may have been hard and harsh at times but the knowledge that I gained was beyond learning from any text books. It was real. Real spiritual knowledge is the only phrase I can place on this and maybe that is something for yourselves to think about unlocking, if you ever have the opportunity. I don't mean going to the main big cities, but finding the real, as I did, the real old gurus and magis, who live in the middle of nowhere. Forget the ones that are in the lights of the big cities now. There are certain "has-beens" and "wannabes" with rather large over-inflated egos, but find the gentle wise man or wise woman in the small village out back. You will be surprised at what knowledge they have and what knowledge they will be willing to pass on to you.'

'Did you have a sense that your footsteps were being guided, or did you feel that it was all by chance?'

'It was all by chance. I wanted to learn, so it was just by talking to the village elders, as you would call them, finding out where the local guru was, or local shaman or wise man and being polite enough to ask for his knowledge or some of his knowledge.'

'So you believed at the time that it was just by chance? Because the older I get the more I realise that there isn't such a commodity.'

'Well, there may have been a greater source steering me but at the time I saw it as just chance.'

'Did you have times when you actively made a choice between going left or right? Did you instinctively feel that you should go that way rather than the other?'

'Yes, as you say I went with my "gut feeling" and as you see, it paid off!'

'You have spoken about a lot of teachers that helped you and taught you their knowledge – the gurus and magi – but did you also learn from your spirit guides and helpers?'

'Yes, I suppose I did.'

'Were you aware of them?'

'Yes, of course, but again with the shaman it is the knowledge that they passed on to me that helped open up a higher connection with the spiritual teachers. So it did come from two sides of the coin. As you know, the more teachers that you have on the physical to assist you to progress higher on the spiritual, the better your knowledge becomes. It is a lovely two-way blend because you become stronger.'

'When you saw the shaman, were you ever taught conflicting things, as if one told you one thing and another told you something that conflicted with that?'

'That is something that I very rarely came across. Maybe some of their ideas may have been slightly different, but there was never anything that was white and black and black and white. There were never any complete contradictions.'

'I mean, for instance, on the earth now there are people who don't believe that there is a negative side to the spirit world and yet there are also people that believe that there is. So this is an example of something that is quite conflicting. '

'Man has created the negativity from those who preach from the pulpits.'

'Although sometimes we can be attacked when we are not thinking about it or inviting it.'

'But there has to be negative to bring the positive back into balance. Even as I see with your electric machines, do you not have to have a positive with a negative? If the negative doesn't exist you cannot have your electricity, my friends. You must have them in balance. Maybe the negative side that has been drummed into you from an early age is the devil or Lucifer. But why should it be? There have been many thousands of, I will call them "devils" – it is easier for me to speak this way – but these come from different cultures of what man has known since he has been walking sensibly on the earth. But again, why do you think there is a negative side? To bring back a balance again?'

'But it's become—'

'Imbalanced.'

'There is too much of the negative now.'

'Again, that is brought about by modern man's greed.'

'There was an occasion, you will verify whether it's true or not, somebody was possessed by the devil and you transferred it into the swine from Gadara and they all jumped into the Sea of Galilee. Is there any truth in this?'

'I wish there was, but the poor man at the time was having a small epileptic fit and with my healing hand and some help from Mary with some herbs, we managed to control him. But in that controlling state there just happened to be a herd of pigs being driven past and in the commotion they panicked and ran off.'

'There is always a logical answer.'

'So logical, yes, my friends, but that is the basis of it. If you turned back the clock to when it happened, when would it have been reported? A hundred years later when the story had been expanded and twisted?'

'It had to be worth telling, didn't it?'

'Of course.'

'I would also think that now we understand mental illness, in those days it was not so well known.'

'Classed as "madness".'

'Yes, classed as madness, so only too readily those pigs came into the picture.'

'But even in your modern terms now, how often does some poor soul have an epileptic fit? Even in your modern streets, how often do people walk and shy away?'

'They probably think he is drunk.'

'Yes, but again look at the commotion it does cause. I know it is not the victim's fault, but it does cause upsets, but not in a spiteful way. It does cause quite a commotion.'

'Last time, JC, we got up to the time just before your crucifixion. Maybe before we go on to that we just need to see if there is anything that you would like to say that we may have missed out last time.'

'I don't know what was said, my apologies.'

'One of the last things that you were talking about was the two last suppers, which happened on the same day.'

'Yes, that's right, and we talked about Judas as well.'

'You said Judas actually got the money but he was betrayed by someone inside who stole the rest of it, left 13 pieces of silver on him and hanged him. You said that it was the priests, or the priests that had him murdered. Why would they implicate Judas? You also said he was singled out because he had a minor criminal record and fitted the bill rather well. You did say it was a distraction as well, did you not?'

'Yes.'

'To take the attention away from you and Mary, is that what you meant?'

'Yes.'

'But it didn't go according to plan.'

'As I said last time, all well-made plans sometimes have a flaw.'

'Because you also were arrested and were hoping to be released at the Passover and that also didn't go to plan.'

'That was down to the hierarchy of the priests who did not like what we were doing. As I have said many times, we were a threat to them.'

'So can you tell us about the next steps that led up to the crucifixion?'

'From where?'

'The last part, when we were talking about Judas, and walking in the Garden of Gethsemane.'

'As I have said, this was all arranged between the three or four of us. There were not many who had known what was to be done. Judas was in on the game. Maybe it wasn't a game but he was in on the master plan. We knew that the priests would think that he would be easily bribed because of his minor criminal record or what he had done in his younger days and because he had been a tax collector, so he volunteered. But we did not expect him to lose his life. We expected him to meet up with myself and Mary when we got to where we were going. But, to this day, we still do not know who did the dirty trick.'

'Were you apprehended shortly after that?'

'Yes.'

'So obviously, it was your intention to "leg it". But Judas, actually, to all intents and purposes, pretended to betray you. So, where were you? Did they apprehend you immediately after this?'

'Yes, they did.'

'Because you were in the wrong place?'

'No, because that is where we had set up to be apprehended, in the garden of Gethsemane.'

'So you at this point had no idea of your fate?'

'As far as we were concerned I was to be to set free on the feast of the Passover. But the hierarchy got their thugs into the crowd and bribed them to call for Barabbas and that is who was freed.'

'And it was at that point that it dawned on you that you were going to be executed?'

'Yes. So there were a few other things quickly put into place.'

'So after the choice was made that you weren't to be released, what happened?'

'I had a visit from Mary and between us we came up with the idea of drugs to kill me off – but not to kill me off!'

'To lower your heart rate and slow your breathing and make it appear as if you are dead?'

'Yes.'

'What sort of anticipation did you have about bleeding to death, because you were pierced by nails? Did you worry about that?'

'Coming back to my lost years and my travels around India, I could go into a meditative state to take away the pain and to cut the bleeding to a very bare minimum.'

'So when then nails went through your arm, you didn't feel anything?'

'Within my travels, I was taught the ability to remove my spirit from my body and not to feel any pain, or to feel the minimum of pain.'

'Did they make you carry your cross to the place of execution? Is that a fact or was it already there?'

'I carried it through the square, not all the way up the hill.'

'Did you have the thorns on your head?'

'Yes.'

'Had you been tortured?'

'No.'

'In the Bible it says that you were scourged, which I presume meant that you were beaten.'

'There were those in the crowd that wanted to spit and throw things and hit, so that was the way it went, I suppose. With the abilities I had, it did not physically hurt me, but maybe emotionally, as there were those that could be so spiteful. However, the Roman soldiers were very compassionate and a lot of them wept with guilt, but were unable to assist or do anything. They were not as spiteful as they have been made out to be in some of the scriptures.'

'They were too fearful to intervene? Well, it was orders, wasn't it? Was the fact that you were sedated quite heavily the reason it was misinterpreted that you were the only son of God? That it was something supernatural because you stood out from humanity? Was this misread?'

'As our friend here knows, a few weeks ago I spoke through this one, but I did not say who I was. I asked the audience did they think that this man had died on the cross for their sins. How could he have done, when he didn't even know you? Isn't it about time you took responsibility for what you have done? So often people blame me or God, rather that facing up to the consequences of what they have done. Again, coming from the hierarchy of the Christian beliefs, I suppose, or the Church beliefs, these things that they had included to unload their guilt onto others.'

'It's a wonderful way to hook people in, isn't it? If somebody is interested in your sins? Payback time!'

As I have said in the past as well, or asked the audience how many people think that when they pass over that St Peter will be sitting by the gates to judge you?'

'I was relying on that!' Laughter.

'Well, I am sure, my friend, I can make arrangements for you.'

'The gates have got to be pearly, otherwise no deal!'

'Would you like the red carpet as well?'

'No, that won't be necessary!' Laughter.

'As I have said, if God loves you all why should he condemn you to hell? He is all loving and all forgiving, so why would he be so spiteful as to send you down there?'

'If there is a down there.'

'Of course.'

'Well, I think that we have created it.'

'In my opinion all those that go "down there" are the hierarchy that bully and punish everybody, particularly those from the churches. I feel that they should be at the front of the queue.'

'With regards to Peter, it is alleged that you said "Thou art Peter. Upon this rock I shall build my church". What is all that about? Did you actually say "church"?'

'No, I preferred to be in the open, to be in God's church. Why do you need a cold building with hard seats to try and talk to somebody that loves you? Why can't you sit on the grass, sit on a rock, sit by the water, sit in his natural church, or his cathedral if you wish? Why does it have to be done inside?'

'Because of the weather! When it was alleged you said that, was it a conspiracy by the Church to back up their legitimacy of the direct descent from you?'

'Yes.'

'Oh, I see. So they alleged that this was another part of your subversive activities to undermine the Church?'

'Why would I want a church if I did not need one?'

'Yet the Church is based on you having been on earth. So, after they took you from the cross, did they put you in the tomb?'

'Yes.'

'So, your plans started from there?'

'A new "Plan B", yes.'

'Can we go back a little? What about the part that Peter played, did he deny knowing you?'

'Yes.'

'Was that part of the plan?'

'No.'

'He denied you three times?'

'Yes.'

'Did you say that it would happen before it did?'

'Yes.'

'When you said that, did you know who it was?'

'Yes.'

'Was it just his fear?'

'A little bit more.'

'His family?'

'Yes. Also, he wasn't as close as has been suggested.'

'So he was one of the people on the outside of the group?'

'How do you mean, my friend?'

'Are you saying that he wasn't one of the closest? Not in the inner circle, but on the outside?'

'Agreed.'

'How did his denial affect you, were you hurt?'

'I knew it would happen.'

'Yes, but still, if I know something will happen and it happens I can still be upset.'

'But I had expected it. Now, what is the right way to put it in your modern terms? If he had been a spy, he would have been a double agent. Does that answer the question for you?'

'So, he was just looking after himself.'

'As many others were as well.'

'Going back to the crucifixion, at what point did Mary give you the drugs to take?'

'It was on the sour wine, on the sponge that the Roman soldier gave me, which we had prepared earlier. And, of course, there was a little bit more on the spear.'

'Oh, right that was clever, wasn't it?'

'We had an idea that this would be done, and to this day, I know that the poor young soldier suffered terrible nightmares, but it is one thing that I do not hold against him. In another way he helped. I suppose you could say he helped me to die.'

'Unknowingly?'

'Yes, unknowingly. He was a part of the plan, but he didn't know what he had done.'

'He didn't know that the end of the spear was "laced"?'

'Laced with a little bit more.'

'But he had the compassion to finish you off.'

'Yes, and from my point of view, it takes a lot of guts and courage to stick by his convictions as he saw them. He had seen it as – forget me being the saviour – he had seen it in a compassionate way, helping a poor soul to die. As we would do with any animal, put them out of their misery very quickly. He had done this and it took a lot of courage, even at his tender age.'

'When you were up there, you spoke to your fellow "executionees", is that right? Were there others?'

'Yes, there were three of us.'

'You managed to give them a reading, as such. One of them was sceptical, apparently?'

'He was frightened more than sceptical. Yet again we come back to what had been drummed into him by the priests. Being that he was a rapist and a murderer, he would be sent or cast into hell, not knowing that his spirit would ascend. I am not saying that he would be forgiven, but be would be encouraged to examine his life and admit the bad that he had done, but there would be nobody there to punish him. This was, I feel, his biggest fear, he was being punished there and then and would he be punished again once he had gone. So you can understand his apprehension.'

'The other one accepted what you said.'

'I just wanted their souls to go home in peace.'

'How long were you up on the cross?'

'It must have been from just coming up to sunset to the early hours of the morning. A lot of our mystic acts had to be done in darkness. It is just something that we had to wait and see.'

'Did the soldiers help to get you down?'

'Yes.'

'Was it them that took you to the tomb?'

'No, that was my family and a few friends. As you know the tomb belonged to someone else, who volunteered to allow us to have it.'

'It must amuse you to see the Turin Shroud, is there a likeness?'

'Similar, yes.'

'Is there any truth in that being your shroud?'

'Why could it not be?'

'Two thousand years is a long time for a piece of material to exist.'

'I was wrapped in one like it to be taken to the tomb, yes.'

'But that wasn't the Turin Shroud?'

'I don't think so, no. It would have to be a miracle to survive.'

'Also to have almost a photographic likeness, it must be the work of an artist.'

'A very clever one.'

'How much were you aware on the cross?'

'I was not. After the drugs kicked in, I suppose as you could say, I was away in cuckoo land. High as a kite on wacky backy! I should not mock, my apologies!'

'Were there crowds still around when they took you down?'

'There were a few still around, most had gone home.'

'And presumably most were your family?'

'Yes.'

'Did you have to be taken down before the Sabbath? So everybody would have gone home?'

'Yes.'

'What about your parents at this stage, were they aware of your fate?'

'What do you mean?'

'Did they receive knowledge that you were arrested, that you were going to be crucified? Did they travel?'

'No.'

'They couldn't. So that must have been very difficult for them?'

'Yes.'

'You allegedly said from the cross to one of your disciples, to your mother, "Here is your mother". You handed her over to James. As if he would now look after her because you couldn't. But if she wasn't there, he couldn't have done that, could he?'

'Again more—'

'Padding?'

'Yes. To cover their tracks and to make what they had done look more compassionate.'

'More Hollywood, isn't it? So, when you were in the tomb, how long did it take you before you came round again?'

'Halfway through the next day, I suppose.'

'Was Mary there waiting for you?'

'Yes.'

'Was there anyone else there?'

'Two or three to help to roll the rather large stone from the front, which is something Mary couldn't have done on her own. No disrespect to the ladies.'

'None taken.'

'There were herbs to counteract inside the tomb. As you know, everything is done by anointing, to assist you with your passage back home. So if people had been nosey and gone looking, all they would have seen is the anointing herbs and things put in there for us. Nobody would have been disrespectful to test them or inspect them. It was a done thing, the way it was done and accepted.'

'So they were herbs to revive you?'

'Yes.'

'I know that you have told us in the past that one of the herbs was Belladonna, and that was the one that took you away from yourself. Do you know what the other herbs were?'

'I cannot remember, maybe you should ask Mary, she was the clever lady with herbs. Very skilful.'

'An ordeal like crucifixion must have left you pretty exhausted and in some pain, I should think. How did they secrete you away from the tomb?'

'I was taken to, what you might say was a "safe house", which was outside the city, for three or four weeks' rest and recuperation.'

'Oh, you stayed there as long as that? I envisaged you being rushed out of the place as soon as—'

'I was within five or six miles of the city. A small place in the middle of nowhere, basically.'

'Yes, well, that seems sensible.'

'There were always visitors to and fro with camel trains, so a stranger would not look out of place.'

I think when you talked about it before you said that you were just laid across a camel or horse, so presumably you weren't that conscious for weeks?'

'I was conscious, but high as a kite, I suppose.'

'Oh, really? Yes, of course. And also probably weak. You had the nails through you. You must have lost a lot of blood.'

'There was still a decent amount lost, I suppose.'

'Something has come to mind, the thing that we know as the Stigmata. Can you say anything about that? Is that actually a phenomenon, or is it something that has been falsified?'

'It is something that has been blown out of context.'

'So you don't think that this relates to you?'

'I feel very angry about this. Why would I come and impose my suffering on others?'

'Not your nature.'

'If I was, as the scriptures and Bible say, like my father, all loving and forgiving, why would I come down and inflict that on others on the earth now? I feel that that would be a spiteful act, not a loving act.'

'Could it be induced by the stigmatised person, because they are never in between the two bones on the forearm, they are always on the palms. That suggests that it is literary a head game. It could be self-induced, because it's in the wrong spot. Were the nails through your arms, then?'

Nods.

'So that's about five inches from the base of the palm, between the two bones, and your feet as well? Were they in your feet or were you tied?'

'I was tied by my feet and had a spike through my forearms. So, again you have answered the question of Stigmata already. Has nobody ever questioned this?'

'It's a miracle!'

'What a miracle that no one has ever questioned it!'

'Well, I am sure that many people have questioned it. Yes, it's hysteria really, isn't it?'

'It's mind over matter.'

'So, after you were packed onto your camel or donkey – was it a camel or a donkey?'

'Donkey.'

'You were then ferried away from the area.'

'As I have said, to a safe house.'

'To allow you to recover. And from there, where?'

'The escape plan was formulated and put into practice, which was very successful, thank you.'

'You obviously travelled in a smaller group than when you went to Turkey and Greece, for the purposes of being incognito. How many were you?'

'There must have been about 20 or 30 of us. We were not that small a group, because a small group of two or three people would have been very conspicuous, but a large camel train, nobody would have taken any notice of whatsoever.'

'So were all those people in that group aware of who you were?'

'No.'

'So, you infiltrated your way into—' laughter. 'But surely it was only important to be incognito in the immediate surroundings? Once you were clear of that, people wouldn't know who you were?'

'No, that's right.'

'So which direction did you take?'

'I went north.'

'Yes, and Mary went south?'

'Yes.'

'So, did the wise man go with you?'

'Yes.'

'Did his wife go with Mary?'

'Yes.'

'So they went to North Africa, Egypt, etc?'

'Yes.'

'And you went...?'

'To Turkey and across the top, to Greece and—'

'That must have taken quite a while. I am assuming that you went to France?'

'From Greece we went by boat.'

'At that particular time, was Mary pregnant?'

'Yes.'

'Did you know at the time?'

'No.'

'Did she arrive in France first? Did you have a destination?'

'We knew where we were going to go.'

'But you still had to find her.'

'Yes.'

'So you had a nice surprise when you did find her?'

Nods.

'I think you said that it took about two years, is that right?'

Shakes head.

'No? How long did it take, then?'

'It must have taken about 14/15 months. As you can quite imagine, I was still in a weakened state.'

'You had to pace yourself.'

'Yes. I would go with one camel train, but at the watering holes or stop off points, I would wait for another to come along. So this is why it took me a while longer. It was just down to me slowly rebuilding my strength. By having a rest for two or three days at a stopover point, it allowed me to gain strength as well and cope with the tiring journey until I was back to full strength again.'

'At some point the camels petered out and changed to—?'

'That's right, yes. It's like your motorway services. Like those, I would rest and one camel train would go on and I would wait to pick up the next one.'

'It must have been quite a relief to go from Greece in a boat after all that trekking?'

'Yes, it was.'

'You went directly to France?'

'Yes. It was only a small, minor port that we went from, in a small or large fishing boat. I don't know which way you would have seen them now, but very inconspicuous. Also, I could turn my hand to fishing, so I worked my passage.'

'But there wasn't any posse after you because it was assumed that you had died? And risen?'

'That is about the only favour that the churches had done for me – saying that my body had risen and gone back to heaven.'

'Did you hear about this?'

'Yes, many months later. As you can imagine the postal system wasn't as efficient as yours is now!'

'That's not saying much!'

'You said many months later you heard about it? So already the story, as such, is huge and beginning to come together. Were there those that had a different opinion? Thinking that you had actually been whisked away, rather than ascended into heaven? Was the general consensus that you did ascend to heaven?'

'It was just a general consensus that I had. Those who knew, I feel played along with the story.'

'Which has been handed down to us, what a wonderful deception? Incredible that it has worked for so long! Nobody has questioned it for 2,000 years.'

'You see, my friend, you say deception, but who has done the deceiving?'

'Yes, of course, you weren't deceptive. Going back to the crucifixion, were you on the cross when you were given the drugs?'

'Yes.'

'So you had to suffer that?'

'But I did have the ability to take my spirit away from my body and withstand pain. You could inflict whatever pain you wanted on the body and get no reaction.'

'I see.'

'And you must not forget either, that I had seen Mary before the crucifixion.'

'So she administered drugs?'

'Just a little bit of something.'

'Just a little bit of something! Did you see Mary as your saviour?'

'How do you mean, my friend?'

'Because she helped you such a lot. I don't know why, but that just came into mind.'

'I suppose in a way, the way you are thinking, yes. But I saw Mary—'

'I mean the fact that she helped you. You couldn't have done it without Mary. She was absolutely crucial to the whole operation.'

'She was somebody... We just loved each other. Would you not do the same for somebody that you loved?'

'Did it ever cross your mind that maybe she wouldn't be allowed access when you were in jail?'

'No, she would have got there somehow, or got things to me somehow or another.'

'So, you really had absolute faith? Do you think the Romans were quite accepting?'

'Like any soldier, I suppose, who was conscripted into the forces, they had to do the job and they did the job and that was it. They had no choice in the matter, so they did it to the best of their ability and if they could turn a blind eye and get away with things, the same as modern man now, they do exactly the same. As I have said, there were good and bad with the Roman soldiers as well. There were some cruel spiteful ones, but on the other hand there were some really lovely, compassionate ones. So you cannot blame them all.'

'Is there anything that we have neglected to speak about that you can think of?'

'I can't think of anything. Did we talk about the last supper?'

'Yes, we did that, very briefly though. You said there were two sittings?'

'One for the outer circle and one for the inner circle, and we weren't sitting round a table like this, as I have seen in many pictures. It would have been sitting on the floor with sprawling cushions with small tables.'

'Do you recall what you ate?'

'Food!' Laughter. 'It was like naan bread, I can't remember the proper name.'

'Unleavened bread?'

'That's the word. With wine, goat's cheese, grapes and dates.'

'Nuts, berries? Laughter.

'Apologies for laughing, somebody just whispered in my ear when you said "Nuts", they said, "Nuts, whole hazel nuts!"' A cheeky little voice.

'I have an idea who that may be. So the topic of the small group was to make plans for whatever was going to happen – plans A, B, C and Z. But what was the topic and the reason for the last supper for the big group, if it was even called the last supper?'

'Just to say our goodbyes.'

'So everybody was aware? What were the larger group aware of?'

'That things would be moving on.'

'Not necessarily that you were going to be arrested?'

'No.'

'Not that you were going to go?'

'As you would use in your modern-days terms, I was going to go abroad teaching, as they would say, "scripture" preaching.'

'Was that relayed to the authorities by someone in that group?'

'More than likely, yes.'

'So now we come to the point where you were on a boat to France and when you got there you were looking for Mary. Did you know the area that you had agreed to meet in?'

'Yes.'

'How long did it take you to find Mary?'

'About a week to ten days, I suppose.'

'Did she have somewhere to live?'

'We did not stay where we had landed.'

'So then where did you go?'

'Just kept a low profile for a few weeks or months and slowly worked our way through France. I suppose, what you call Southern France now. We felt drawn towards the mountains.'

'Montségur?'

'That's basically where we settled, and where we started our Church – which is the wrong word – but just doing our little things that we had always done: talking to people, healing people, passing on our knowledge, having outside meetings.'

'People were quite accepting?'

'Yes.'

'When you met Mary off the boat, she had a child with her.'

'Yes.'

'What would it have been, about six months old?'

'Maybe nearer a year.'

'Was it a boy or a girl?'

'What do you think?'

'It's got to be one or the other.'

'Can only be half right or half wrong.'

'A girl.'

'Yes.'

'I think you had another one fairly soon afterwards.'

'Yes a son, just after we settled properly.'

'There is a place called Brittany in France where there is an old cathedral dedicated to St Anne, who was allegedly Mary's mother. Is there any truth or any basis for this, or is it pure myth?'

'Could be...'

'Did she come with you?'

'No, but there could be some truth in it – that it was dedicated to her.'

'Dedicated?'

'Yes. You know how stories get out of hand.'

'You said that Mary's father was aware that she went to France?'

'Her father was aware but she was a free spirit anyway. He never knew exactly where she was.'

'So he wasn't sure?'

'He wasn't exactly 100% sure that's where she had gone. He knew that she was a free spirit and I wouldn't say totally uncontrollable, but a very independent single-minded woman. He knew that she was like a wild stallion and you couldn't harness it and the best thing you can do is let them go and be free for themselves.'

'Was the wise man with you still?'

'No.'

'Did he stay in Greece?'

'Yes.'

'Was there anyone else with you?'

'No.'

'Was there anyone with Mary?'

'There was one or two with Mary to help her with the child as well. The wise man's wife had left her in Egypt, where she sailed across back home to Greece. But Mary was on her final leg home, or to her new home.'

'What was your son's name?'

'I cannot remember at the moment.'

'Can you remember your daughter's name?'

'Not at the moment, no. Does it matter?'

'No, just a matter of interest. When you got on the boat to go to France, the wise man had left you and you were completely on your own. Had you regained your strength?'

'Yes, I had regained my strength.'

'So therefore, you were able to help with the fishing?'

'And the running of the boat in general.'

'So there were still some people back in Jerusalem that knew you had left? '

'Two or three.'

'But they kept quiet? Did they come and join you at any particular point?'

'They did visit us later on, many years later, when the dust had settled.'

'Did your parents then learn that you were still alive?'

'Never.'

'How sad for them.'

'It would have been too dangerous for them.'

'Oh, yes, for them to visit, but I thought someone would have just said, "He's all right. He's a long way away, but he's all right." You couldn't get a message to them? No, guess it would have been too risky.'

'Can you imagine what would have happened to them? Not so much the Romans, but what the Church leaders would have done? And I would have had a huge bounty on my head, and my children's heads.'

'Is it something that you really thought a lot about?'

'How do you mean?'

'To not let them know that you were alive must have been quite difficult for you?'

'But it was made up when I passed to spirit and when they had passed too.'

'They would have found out then?'

'There was no animosity there. They understood why and they knew exactly why we had done what we did.'

'Did you sense them around you, when you were still on the earth and they had passed?'

'Of course.'

'So we've now got this new life in France. What sort of age?'

'Oh, goodness me. I suppose I would have been in my early 40s.'

'Perhaps we should leave this now until next time as you are getting tired. Thank you.'

'If there are any other questions at any time please ask.'

'I just want to say, so ingrained has the myth been in my head that I am kind of looking for confirmation. It's a real revelation that things were so different!'

'Thank you for being so honest, I appreciate it. So now you can see why you were spoken to in the past and asked if you were ready and willing to take up the mantel.'

Chapter Four

Life After Death

'Well, here we are again, round four! We finished last time where you arrived in France, and you found Mary and you were headed towards the mountains and you settled near Montségur. Would it have been called that at that time?'

'I do not remember what it was called, I will be honest, we were, in your terms, 30 or 40 miles from the mountains. Why is Montségur significant to you?'

'Because we know that the Cathars were something to do with the after effects of you.'

'The aftermath of my real death.'

'Yes, your influence in other words, and I believe that the Cathars were in the town at Montségur. We did refer to that before. Linguistically it wouldn't have been called that in those times, because the French language was much later on. When the Romans left, it would have been a Latin place in the south of France. French hadn't been invented, it became bastardised from Latin. Linguistically that's what I was saying, that's why you can't remember it, because it would have been named something else.'

'Thank you, my friend, that was explained very nicely, thank you. May we just call it "The Castle" at the moment?'

'So, can you tell us a bit about your home and your life in this area?'

'Yes.'

'Will you?'

'What do you wish to know?'

'How did you settle, you settled near the mountains, but what sort of home did you have?'

'It was not like one of your modern two-up and two-down, it was a smallholding, again in your modern terms you would have called it a small farm.'

'It must have taken you quite a while to recover from your wounds and stuff like that. After that, did you take up a living or profession that was extra to your teaching?'

'No, that was all we did. The smallholding, selling vegetables and livestock on, was just enough to keep us, and to do the extra teachings of what we wanted.'

'Were you good at it, the smallholding?'

'In the end, yes, it took us a while to get the hang of things, but the people, farmers and other folk around us were very helpful.'

'So you were quite well accepted and assimilated into that society?'

'Yes.'

'How did you get the smallholding? You just took over the land, said "I am going to have this bit"?'

'We bought it of course.'

'So you had money?'

'Do you think that we would have fled without any?'

'Gold, frankincense and myrrh.'

'We would not have fled and been penniless.'

'So you bought the smallholding?'

'It had a small house for us, big enough to bring up two children.'

'Did you notice the difference in climate between where you came from and there, and was it a problem?'

'It took me a while to acclimatise, but with the trauma and with what I had been through with the crucifixion, it was better for my health in that way, clearer, cleaner, fresh air.'

'And probably a lot more water, if you were near the mountains, than you had ever seen in your life.'

'It was a health bonus as well, I suppose, to say that I could walk to the mountains and sit and be quiet and be myself.'

'Yes, and, I suppose, the longer it took food to corrupt helped you as well, because where you came from milk doesn't last a day.'

'Yes, that's right, it was a healthier lifestyle for us, which did assist the healing process and even the trauma of healing the mind, for both of us.'

'Can I go back to the people around you? They accepted you, but did they accept you because they knew who you were and what your work was, or because they were well disposed towards foreign people?'

'They were the latter, yes. They accepted me for who I was, rather than what I was doing, because most of them in the area where we were, were people who had moved on and wanted to settle to a new life.'

'Ok, so you felt part of it?'

'We were all strangers in one way, but friends in another way.'

'So, were there people there that you knew?'

'No.'

'Did you do any of your carpentry?'

'A small amount, yes.'

'But I think last time you said you did it for relaxation, probably making toys for the children.'

'That's right, small things, just to pass some time and to help others. Occasionally, I would make or repair furniture for the community, but we were not what you would call a close-knit community, we were spread over many miles, or in your modern-day terms, we did not live like you do now, very close to each other. Does that make some sense?'

'This is a very small question, but it interests me. You did some carpentry, did you bring your own tools or did you come to terms with the difference of tools? Were you able to work in the way that they worked?'

'Yes, I had to restock and adapt.'

'It must have been a wonderful experience seeing tools that you had never seen before.'

'Yes, it was.'

'So, you must have travelled very light when you left, barely able to look after yourself really?'

'We just left with what clothes we had on our backs and what we could just manage, and purchasing what we needed along the way as well.'

'Yes, but you managed to take some money with you, so you must have planned that for some time before.'

'Yes, would you disappear from where you are and not take any money?'

'No.'

'There you are, you see.'

'In the first years when you were in what is now called France, were you visited by people from where you came from?'

'No, it was an agreed thing that we would not meet up because of fear and danger for my family.'

'Did you keep your name the same?'

'What do you think?'

'I think you would have done.'

'It did not matter, because as I said, the little community where we settled, there were people from all other regions. How can I put it in your modern terms? It was as if they wanted to escape from the big cities to live a peaceful life away from all the hustle.'

'What we call an alternative society.'

'They just wanted the freedom to be themselves.'

'Was the area you were in under the tutelage of the Romans?'

'No, well, we were, but we were quite a way away and they did not bother us.'

'No, because I can see problems if the Roman authorities knew you were executed and that you had sprung up somewhere else. They would want to have another go at you.'

'I can quite imagine whoever had found or taken my head would have been hailed a hero. But that is why we settled in this community because they were, I suppose, refugees who wanted to escape from the world that they had been forced to live in.'

'The nails must have caused very visible scars for you once they were healed. Did that ever arouse anybody's suspicion that you were, loosely termed, an escaped criminal?'

'No, because I used to wear leather straps, like you call wristbands, and working on the farm and doing carpentry I could still have said that my chisels had slipped.'

'In a most symmetrical way!'

'But again, most of who were not used to carpentry would not have understood. And again if they had seen the scar here, I could have passed it off as a war wound.'

'What was the scar there, the spear? So that was in your side?'

'Yes, that is the one we have spoken about where the young man did it with the best heartfelt intent.'

'You didn't say where it was before, so it was in your right side, and the spear had herbs, drugs to anaesthetise you?'

'There you are, you see. But again as you know, even in your world now you can explain things away to people in a way that they will understand, but in a way that they do not need to know your business.'

'Can I ask you something very pertinent to me? I was raised as a Catholic and I took on a confirmation name, which happened to be Longinus, the one that speared you. Is there any particular reason why I chose that, I think I am seeing something interesting happening here?'

'Why do you think that you took on that name?'

'Compassion, I think that the soldier saw you for what you were.'

'I will ask you one question back: Do you feel that you could have been that young Roman soldier?'

'Yes, sometimes I do.'

'I will not give you the answer yet.'

'Well, if it was I won't do it again!'

'Maybe you can, when you have the opportunity to meditate and ask, I know you will get the answer. All I can say is that if it was you, thank you very much.'

'It was a pleasure!'

'I am sorry that I may have disappointed your friends around, but I feel that this is a quest that our friend may find the answer for himself. I feel that he knows the answer, but he is very wary of accepting the answer. Like myself, it is a journey that you must make yourself. I do not wish to short change or upset the rest. I feel sure that if they were to meditate, they will find the answers as well. As I said, I have been talking to the wise one and he has suggested a few little things like this for you, maybe to help you to understand yourselves.'

'Who is the wise one?'

'Who did you think it was, my child?'

'I thought it was Merlin. I just wanted to make sure!'

'He told me that I would have trouble with you! A really lovely, wise, gentle character and I feel that it has been more of a privilege to get to know him, more so since I have been speaking to you all through this one. I had been around him in the spirit realms but never had a closeness like there is now.'

'So you are working towards a common cause. Merlin seems to guide so many projects and new ideas.'

'Apologies for going off track a little bit, any other questions?'

'No, it's very interesting. Going back to the smallholding, did you see your life out there?'

'Yes, we did.'

'And your children, did they remain there or did they move on?'

'My son moved on and my daughter married locally and stayed within ten to fifteen miles of where we were.'

'So you were still alive when she married?'

'Yes.'

'Did you have grandchildren?'

'Yes.'

'Did your son marry?'

'Yes.'

'Did he have children?'

'No, he didn't.'

'Was there a reason for that, or they chose not to, or it just didn't happen?'

'It just didn't happen. I feel that he was not meant to have children.'

'I just wondered if there was a problem or he died early or something, but, it just didn't happen. So, your daughter, did you approve of her choice of husband?'

'Why would I not?'

'Well...not all fathers do.'

'But you must not forget that I was not how I was written about. As long as my children were happy, I did not mind. He was a good man.'

'You were not judgemental?'

'Why should I have been? People had been judgemental to me in the past and maybe in one way it was a lesson for me, to accept others how they are. Many times I have spoken about this to many hundreds and thousands of people.'

'In the society where you were, was it a matriarchal or patriarchal society that you landed in what we now call France?'

'It was patriarchal.'

'So, it was quite similar to the one you left?'

'Yes, and I feel that is why so many emigrated from the towns to get away from the stigma and the rules "you must, you must, you must". They wanted freedom, like me I suppose, to be themselves.'

'And in this community, you all treated each other with equality?'

'Yes, we respected each other and we helped each other when we could. We even respected each other's different religious beliefs.'

'What was the prevailing religious belief when you were alive, dear?'

'Catholicism or what you would call Catholicism now. But most of them were, like me, rather Paganistic.'

'I think that we are all looking rather confused now, to think how the prevailing religion could have been Catholicism.'

'Why?'

'Because that comes from the Christianity which was based upon you being at the centre of that Church.'

'But was that not going before I became, as they put it, the head?'

'Was it? Well, obviously this is what we don't know, and this is something very significant.'

'Well, what religion were the Romans? They definitely were not Jewish.'

'I don't know.'

'Catholic, what we call Catholic now, it may not have been call Catholicism then, but I am trying to explain in your modern terms for you.

'Catholic in the sense that the Catholics worshipped idols, is that what you mean?'

'Yes, I do not wish to confuse you with your modern views of Catholicism, which is what I feel you are doing, which you must not.'

'So, why the word Catholic?'

'Because that is the word I can use which you will understand.'

'It means universal. It's interesting that the Cathars are named similar to the Catholics.'

'As you know I had no real religious beliefs from what I had learnt in Greece and on my travels, and again in your modern terms, I was more of a Pagan, respecting nature, and asking for good harvests and thanking for good harvests. Just going back to being at one with nature.'

'And perhaps gardening in the different phases of the moon, harvesting, reaping, sowing...'

'It's all a part of it, yes.'

'Going back to when you were young and you sat with the elders back in the Middle East, is that the sort of theories that you were putting across to them, because they obviously had an extremely rigid taboo-type faith?'

'Yes.'

'And did they? Were they closed to it?'

'As I tried to explain to them, I can understand having, as they would call, a God, but, why can't we have many other Gods, for the seasons, for other things that we do and work with, and why are they not under the control of the main God? Why does there only have to be one?'

'I see. By Gods do you mean areas, special areas of expertise and responsibility? Like, for instance, maybe the Archangels each have a different job to do. Is that what you mean?'

'Yes, why can't you have a God for the harvest, one for each of the seasons? Why does it always have to be one rather than one in charge of many? This is what they could not understand and they did not wish to know.'

'So was this part of your preaching when you were preaching?'

'Talking to many thousands, yes.'

'That was in France, but also before that, was this also part of your preaching then?'

'I would not call it preaching, no.'

'Ok, talking.'

'Thank you, because to me preaching is telling people what to do and "you must". This was to say "look, examine, and if you can take this, take away what you can. Go and use it for your own benefit and the benefit of others."'

'Yes.'

'I do not wish to sound angry there.'

'No, but I didn't take you as being someone who is dictatorial at all.'

'That's the word I was trying to come up with.'

'I would take you more as someone who would want to always encourage others to think about things, maybe sow a few seeds, and maybe prod them into action, to think about things, rather than—'

'Yes, that is the way to live. Again, like myself taking on the smallholding, I had never worked with goats and sheep, or cows. It was a new project for me to learn and assess and use my knowledge and my skills. So again, I gained knowledge by talking to those around me, asking for their assistance and then doing things the way I thought it should be done by using some of their methods.'

'Yes, we have spoken about the language, that it was not the French that we know now, so was it a problem for you?'

'What, to speak Latin?'

'So, it was Latin, you spoke Latin? So there was no problem?'

'Latin was quite a universal language then.'

'Was it? I didn't think it was in the Middle East.'

'The Romans conquered most of the world, so Latin would have been more widely spoken than it is now.'

'It wouldn't have been a high Latin, it would have been a low Latin – colloquial, yes. And each region—'

'Would have had their own slant on the language order, very much like your modern-day dialect of wherever you go within the world.'

'In your days of living in France, did you ever hanker for where you were born, did you ever have feeling of "I wish I could go back and visit xyz"?'

'At times, but not very much. I suppose you could say that I was still mentally scarred from what had happened and I did not wish to venture down that road again.'

'I can see that, but it didn't stop you from thinking and talking to people about it where you were. So even though you were mentally scarred because of the authorities being frightened of what you were doing, you were still prepared to do it again. Did you have any difficulties with any authorities in France?'

'No, they were too busy doing their own thing, I suppose.'

'Did you have any difficulties with the churches where you were in France?'

'There were none close, apart from miles and miles away.'

'Right.'

'As I said, the people who were around where we settled were very much like ourselves and they wanted to break from what they would have called the normal.'

'When you went there did you know where you were going, or did people you knew research where you needed to be?'

'No, we just went from town or village to village until we found somewhere that was…very much like you do now, when you feel somewhere is home, you stay.'

'Yes, okay. So did you talk to people about your experiences in Jerusalem?'

'Some of them, which was all a part of my, "teaching" is not the right word, my "talking" and my "philosophy", I suppose.'

'But you were not specific about what had gone on in Jerusalem, surely to goodness?'

'I spoke as if I had known of a friend who my personal experience had happened to but I did not say that it was me on the receiving end. That was a way of passing on but not arousing too much suspicion.'

'Did you enjoy the relatively quieter life that you had?'

'Yes, it was nice to be, I suppose you would say in the countryside, doing my own thing, enjoying life and my family.'

'Was there a school available for your children?'

'No, we started a school.'

'You started a school, how lovely!'

'For the local community and it was something that we all put our little skills into, to give the children a basic education.'

'Oh, how lovely!'

'Nothing too hard and dogmatic or too religious, but the basics from all the knowledge that we all had.'

'So, did you run this school from your smallholding?'

'No, it was run a bit further away from us. As I say, it was a community effort and the whole community got involved.'

'Did you teach alternative stuff, not the standard, whatever was dished out?'

'Yes, and so did Mary.'

'Was this the start of the Cathars?'

'I suppose it could have been the general unfolding of it. If it was the start it, I will say, was not started deliberately as a group of people.'

'But you were teaching these children to think the same way that you were thinking and other people around were thinking.'

'I was offering a way to think. The way I was thinking. I would not teach, I would not push my beliefs on anyone.'

'Okay, there were other people in the community that had similar ideas and views to you, so therefore it would have been quite acceptable for their children to have been given this knowledge or information. So it would have been right, but it would have also caused a generation to grow up thinking the same way as you and the people around you.'

'Maybe not thinking the same way, but being very open minded in the way that they looked at the world. As your friend Merlin would say, "Think out of the box", and this is what we opened their minds to do, to think beyond the boundaries of what people wanted you to.'

'Was music and singing part of it? Did you involve your children with music? Did you have music? What kind did you have?'

'We had basic flutes or pipes and lyres or, um...I cannot think of the right word for them.'

'Harps?'

'Harps and, of course, Mary taught them, more so the harp and the lyre. I was not very musical myself, but would join in and make a noise. There were many others, for the sake of me talking, may I use the word community? Within the community where we were, there were those that had musical skills. So again, it was all moulded together. Those children that were that way inclined were encouraged, and whatever skills the children could turn their hands to, if they enjoyed these tasks, they were encouraged more. None were forced to play a musical instrument if they did not have the desire, but if there was one with a desire to learn about the cattle and the sheep, somebody would take him under his wing and give him the experience of learning, rather than forcing him into each little block of what they should have done.'

'Were they taught too about the herbs and medicines in that way?'

'Yes. For those that wished to learn this, would come along and see Mary. So, as I said, those with the interest and special skills were given extra tuition or extra help in whatever they had the desire and wish to learn. There were many that wanted to dip their toe in every piece to have a little bit of knowledge of everything.'

'Was reading and writing taught?'

'Yes.'

'Could you read and write?'

'Of course!'

'Well, I don't know. You could have been taught by word of mouth, talking.'

'I know what you mean, my friend.'

'I know you went to school, but was it like it is now, basic teaching then?'

'No.'

'No, so it was a bit hit and miss as to whether you could read and write then?'

'This is where my friend the wise man taught me much when I went to Greece.'

'Could your parents read and write?'

'Maybe not as good as a lot of others, but they could. It seems to be quite a myth that people who were born in my time were illiterate. Why does modern man seem to think that he is the only clever one to have walked the earth?'

'But then, what I just said to you about the schooling being a bit hit and miss, so therefore it wasn't always available?'

'I am not saying that everyone had schooling, but those who desired could, and those that had money could pay the priests to teach.'

'So you are saying that there was a bigger percentage that could read and write than what modern man thinks there was?'

'Maybe their reading and writing was not perfect in your terms of today, but they all, a lot of them, had the basic skills to read and write.'

'Could you speak English when you were on the earth, did you ever go to any English speaking areas?'

'No, again English would not have been spoken the way that you speak now.'

'No, I understand that, but you never came across the language?'

'Only when I met up with Mary.'

'So Mary could speak it?'

'Well, she came through England had she not?'

'Right, but it doesn't necessarily mean that she—'

'She had picked up some English on her travels through, it may not have been a great big dictionary full of it, but there were some words and phrases.'

'So going back to the schooling, that must have really been a wonderful way of life and ideal for your children, knowing that they were taught the values of life.'

'Yes.'

'So, when they left home and went to do their own thing, you said that your son moved away. So where did he go, do you know?'

'He went back to our birthplace, to the Middle East as you call it.'

'Oh, did he? Why did he do that?'

'Because that was his choice, he was an adventurer.'

'Curious, did he know your early life story?'

'Yes.'

'Did he want to explore?'

'He wanted to go and look.'

'Did he go and see your parents?'

'They would not have been alive then.'

'No, of course not. So did he go and visit anyone else that you would have known?'

'I did not tell him about people I had known. I would have had to lie to him in that way to protect him.'

'So was there still a danger there then, when he went?'

'Well, there may have been, yes.'

'So, you never ever landed in England with your uncle, as the fable goes, not in Glastonbury?'

'Mary did, but I did not.'

'Was there a reason why she went there?'

'It was her route across to France.'

'So that was her only reason?'

'Why else would she have come to a cold isle?'

'For the food!'

'She did stay there for a few weeks or few months, in a monastery, I think it was, for a little bit of rest and recuperation.'

'Was the baby born here, in Glastonbury?'

'Um hum.'

'Ah, interesting, so, just going back to your son: he went off adventuring, did he come back? You never saw him again, no? Did you hear from him? Do you know what happened to him?'

'Yes.'

'Can you tell us?'

'He died in a skirmish with the Syrians.'

'So, quite young, then?'

'He was in his 30s, or late 20s, early 30s. But he had done what he wished to do, and I know from some of the letters that we had that he had a good life, but that is all that matters. He achieved what he wanted, and again, he went with our blessings.'

'Last time you couldn't remember his name, has that memory come back?'

'It hasn't, I will apologise to you there, I will have to rack my brain and let you know.'

'I am sorry. I don't mean to upset you in any way. Your daughter, did she live to a ripe old age?'

'I presume she did.'

'Well, you would have known, by the fact that you would have seen from the spirit world. So how many children did she have?'

'Five.'

'That's nice. Were you alive to see all of them?'

'No.'

'How many children did you see?'

'Four.'

'Boys or girls?'

'Yes!'

'Two of each!'

'Five, one must have been half of something and half of something else!'

'Yes, must have been!'

'Three girls and two boys.'

'You said that you weren't alive to see the last one, so how old were you when you passed back to spirit?'

'I suppose in my 70s, as you would say in your modern terms.'

'And how old was Mary?'

'A similar age, we went within a few months of each other. It was not like many that I have seen when a partner dies and ten, twenty or thirty years later the other one dies, it was only a matter of months.'

'Can you tell me, is your line still active today, are your descendants still walking this planet?'

'I would sincerely hope so.'

'That's wonderful! There has been a lot of emphasis put on this lately, which has been kept secret for a long time to protect the descendants, is this true?'

'That would be nice if it was, but how could they keep records?'

'Some have said that the Cathars were protecting the descendants, is that right?'

'Could very well have been.'

'But you are not going to tell me.'

'Not at the moment, no.'

'I want to try and understand why they would still be in danger, your descendants.'

'From the Catholic Church.'

'They would be called heretics, wouldn't they? And they would be out to have their blood.'

'And we can't have anyone putting them down, can we, taking away their power?'

'Do you know if your descendants now know that they are your descendants?'

'No, they do not know, it has been 2,000 years.'

'It must be very diluted.'

'Thank you, my friend, yes.'

'Do you know who they are?'

'Not all of them.'

'Some of them?'

'As our friend says, it must be very diluted. What is to say that some of these people are five people sitting round this table here?'

'I think that it is clear that it is not important to you, so why has this been blown up publicly? Is it something that has been done to stir the churches up?'

'Control. Done by the churches because they are losing control and they want the control back. So, what better way to start a rumour about something entirely different? So, while they can beaver away in the background looking for the truth, everyone else is running around like headless chickens, looking for the heads.' Birds in the background. 'Yes, my friend, I would agree with you. So, does that make sense?'

'Yes.'

'The propaganda is put out by the churches because they are frightened. The masses run round like headless chickens and the churches sit back and look for the truth at their own ease. Simple but effective.'

'So, just to go back, has your daughter's name returned to you?'

'Has my daughter's name returned?'

'Have you remembered?'

'Oh, sorry, I am sure that we called her Mariah, which was very similar to her mother's name, but a little bit different, and maybe, where we were settling, it did not look so conspicuous.'

'Thank you.'

'You seem to be stuck for questions.'

'Not really, it's processing it really, because it's all so amazing.'

'Why is it so amazing, my friend?'

'Because it's the kind of territory that everyone will be so fascinated with, it's the greatest—'

'But nobody dares tread.'

'No.'

'But as I have said to you from when we started talking properly, I was no different to you or any of you sitting round this table, I was just a man doing what I loved to do. It was other, I will call them idiots, in higher places of the churches that wanted to take this away and make something special of it, in order to control and enhance the masses.'

'And they did make something of it – they made a huge thing of it and have done for thousands of years.'

'And what did they do with those who would not listen and would not take them on board?'

'Get rid of them.'

'Murder them.'

'Of course, they used the old adage of witchcraft. They were witches, so we have a right to destroy them. Ruling by fear, isn't it?'

'Have they not always done that?'

'When you were in France did you do any writing? Did you have any manuscripts or writings for people to—?'

'No, it was all done by word of mouth. You start putting things on papyrus they get lost and appear somewhere else in the world and all of a sudden you have the world and his dog sitting in your back garden, either wanting to kill you or wanting to know more about you, and your peace is gone.'

'Did you hear about any of the people that you had left behind doing any writing or putting anything down?'

'Some of them did I heard, yes.'

'The disciples?'

'Or as they would call them in your modern terms, the Apostles. But how many times has their writing been changed to suit the fools that want to control the masses?'

'During your lifetime, did stories reach you about this person Jesus and the crucifixion?'

'Um hum.'

'What sort of stories? Were they exaggerated?'

'Of course. About this so called "soul" that was crucified on the cross and was put in a tomb and the next day he was out, ascended to heaven in a fiery chariot.'

'Oh, he was in a fiery chariot too, there was a lot of them about then, wasn't there!'

'It was the accepted form of transport!'

'Just like Elijah really. It beats camels and donkeys!'

'There you see how stories get exaggerated, and of course the Romans panicked because I had disappeared and just like your modern-day police looking for criminals, they go round to their known haunts or where they had been and that was it.'

'They couldn't find you?'

'Because nobody knew where I had gone.'

'Does that mean that a lot of Romans were converted to Christianity because you disappeared then reappeared, or did they think that you had escaped?'

'I do not see where you are. Do you mean, were they converted to Christianity? Why should they be instantly converted because I had disappeared?'

'No, because you were saying that the stories were coming to you, that you had left the tomb and that you reappeared in front of various disciples and that you ascended to heaven in a fiery chariot. Did they accept that or did that then change their way of thinking?'

'Why should that change their way of thinking?'

'Because they weren't thinking that way, were they? They weren't thinking of you as the saviour then, that's really what I mean.'

'No, this is something that came in many years later, it didn't happen overnight like making stock, it took many hundreds of years before they decided to cash in on the story. It wasn't overnight, because I was crucified the next day, they were all converted. Mind you, that is the way it says in some of the books, I'm sure, but it didn't happen that way.'

'Of course it didn't. So the Romans went on a sort of witch hunt, trying to track you down?'

'But because there was no trace, they had to accept.'

'They had to accept that there was a mystery there.'

'Um hum. But again they had more important things to do than to chase around the world for somebody who had disappeared.'

'Someone they didn't think was guilty in the first place. I was just thinking what you said earlier about the content of what you were telling people. It was a conversation that was brought up before. We were thinking that perhaps next time we would elucidate, you know, explain what kind of things you were talking to people about, like you just said. For instance, not being judgemental, taking people as they are and that kind of stuff. We were just chalking that up for a possibility next time.'

'So, the fact that you went round talking to people, in the Middle East I am talking about, did that have a real affect and change things? Because it was as though the churches tried to resist by getting rid of you, but had you already sown the seeds? Were the people there starting to question?'

'They were starting to. They were starting to think for themselves.'

'Do you think that what you did made a difference?'

'Yes, as I have said earlier, in other times that we have spoken, I was classed as being quite radical. But I did not wish to stir up the masses to have riots, I just wanted people to think for themselves, to stop and look at something. Rather than taking everything for granted, be grateful for what small things you have.'

'So this making a difference, then, do you feel that it was the start of changes happening?'

'Yes.'

'Which is what you started out to do really, so you succeeded?'

'I feel that I succeeded.'

'Do you think that, because you were crucified and rose to heaven, it made people think more about what you had said?'

'But I didn't rise to heaven.'

'No, but they thought you had.'

'Yes, but again the biggest problem there, with the churches getting the story, they turned a myth into an even bigger myth.'

'Can't put it back in the box.'

'By saying that I was the only one that could do that, nobody else can do it. Do you not all return to heaven, as you call it, when you pass over?'

'Yes.'

'Well, there you are.'

'If you've been good boys and girls! I like to think, even if we have not been.'

'I would agree with you, my friend.'

'We know that we do, I was just mocking.'

'But again, the stranglehold of what we have, coming back to the start point again, the churches wanting total control.'

'Which is slipping from their fingers these days, is it not?'

'Yes, at a fast rate of knots, I feel.'

'So maybe this time is particularly appropriate.'

'Well, it seems to me that there are various books that have come out about your life, about how you may not have died. I'm thinking of the Dan Brown books. Okay, they are meant to be fiction and that may be how they have got out, but it just seems to be that these things tend to come out in different quarters, in different ways, but all at the same time. Is that going to be the same with us with what we are doing, that this is reiterating what it is already starting to be put out there but this is much more in depth?'

'Not being rude to your Dan Brown's writings, but in one way you could take his writing as being like a true fairy story. But again, please do not think that I am mocking this man. What you and we are doing here, is like some of the writings, like some of his books, the foundations for you to build on and to present.'

'Well, it was quite a thing at the time when the books came out. It made people think.'

'Of course, that is the idea. I have seen some of his writings when I have been overlooking many, and what I have seen is something quite wonderful, because he is coming back to what our good wise one Merlin says. He is making people think out of the box, and is that not a good thing for anybody, living and an education? That is what so many of the Church leaders do not like, because people are starting to think and question. Why should you not question your local priest or vicar if there is something that you have been talking with him about and don't agree with? It does not mean that you should take up violence. Why should you not have a good argumentative discussion and question his beliefs, as he would be the first to question yours? So that is a good thing about these writings.'

'But I mean that a lot of his writings have been based on what other people were inspired to say as well. For instance, DaVinci, I wonder if he was spirit inspired. I mean inspired to drop these pearls of knowledge.'

'And why not? These pearls had been dropped many years ago and they have just started to take root and grow. So he is opening up the door, or rolling out the carpet for you to start your journey.'

'It's been a fascinating journey so far.'

'I am pleased that it is helping you to understand things in a roundabout manner.'

'Yes, well, now we don't believe in all the fables that we have been taught, I never could swallow them, even as a child. It has been so refreshing to have your—'

'To hear it from the horse's mouth?'

'Yes, absolutely! Did the wise man and his wife ever come to see you in France?'

'Yes, they did once. It was about four years after we had settled and got our community together.'

'Oh, good! Did you ever go to Greece to visit them? '

'No.'

'You considered that to be too dangerous?'

'Too close to home, or old home, I should say.'

'Because they didn't come all the way with you, did they?'

'No.'

'They put you on a boat?'

'Put us on a boat and made sure that Mary got away safely. And, I suppose, our friend would have left her at Libya, and then she could go straight across the Mediterranean back home to Greece and Turkey.'

'Last time you said that you thought that it was Egypt.'

'Yes, well, it is close.'

'Then "Mrs" wise man wouldn't have seen the baby?'

'Only when they came to see us.'

'Why did Mary go to England, instead of where she was going to meet you?'

'It was safer for me to travel north on my own and for Mary to travel south on her own. We would have been less conspicuous. They may have been looking for a couple, especially as I had disappeared and Mary had left Jerusalem, so it was to fool them, if you understand.'

'Yes, I understand.'

'It was safer for Mary and our family, and me.'

'We have talked about your family and your children, and the fact that you had five grandchildren, but there must have been other friends and acquaintances that you made that had an affect on your life and maybe helped you in what you did. You mentioned about this community, but did you venture away from that community to do any talking to people?'

'Occasionally, we would go further out to the bigger towns, to the markets, to trade goods and get supplies for ourselves. To trade what we had an excess of and we would talk to many people then. Because, I will call it a community, they would know people from the towns and cities that they had left, and they would enquire of how their new life in the country is going. Many were interested in healing and herbs and other things that we had to say and we would talk and we would go to their houses and they would gather a few friends around and we would even have communication with spirit. But that was only done for those who, like you do now, wanted to know and liked these things. We kept quite a low profile, so we did other small things like that as well. It wasn't just sitting at home on the farm doing nothing.'

'I'm sure. So this is part of the picture, we start off with the family and we move out and find out about other people in your life. Did you ever venture outside of France?'

'No.'

'So you stayed within—'

'Stayed within the boundaries of France.'

'But you went to some of the big cities or towns?'

'Bigger towns, yes, once we got braver, because we became part of the countryside. The more we became part of the countryside, the less conspicuous we became.'

'What did you die from, what caused your death or passing?'

'Stopping breathing!'

'Really!'

'Old age.'

'Just worn out?'

'There was no such thing as pneumonia or cancer or whatever terms of phrase you use, it was just old age and worn out.'

'Presumably, it was the time that you said you were going, before you came?'

'You've lost me, my friend.'

'It was just a thought that we agree before we come here, we decide how long we will stay.'

'Oh, I see what you mean.'

'And I'm sure that it was no coincidence that Mary and you went within months of each other. That's all I was thinking. You were very fortunate in that respect, I must say.'

'I guess after what you had suffered, there was no point in a further separation.'

'It must have been very hard for your daughter to lose both her parents within such a short space of time.'

'But she was like us, she understood.'

'Was she aware of spirit?'

'Uh hum.'

'So you were able to speak to her and reassure her?'

'If you can put it in that term of phrase, she carried on that side of the family name. She knew she wasn't losing us because she knew that she could communicate with us, and vice versa.'

'If it's all right with everybody, I think we will leave it there, unless you have got anything more you want to say.'

General thanks.

Chapter Five

Jesus the Man

'Welcome.'

'Thank you – and you were saying?'

'We were wondering what you talked to people about.'

'All the local gossip – what do you mean, what did I talk about?'

'What sort of philosophy? What were you teaching?'

'I was teaching nothing, but I was talking about how man should respect the earth, respect everything he had, not to be jealous of what others had and in one way, to forget. Not to "forget", that is the wrong word, I'm trying to think of the right word for you. Not to forget that you can still communicate with the spirit realms.'

'Had they forgotten about it, then?'

' It was slowly being forgotten.'

'Just purely for the priesthood. Were they a very materialistic society?'

'They were getting materialistic, yes.'

'In spite of the fact that they went to the temple and all that spiritual PT?'

'But they had lost their spirituality, I suppose, in a way.'

'Do you feel that you were successful in touching some people?'

'Yes, many of those who came and gathered to see us, if you want to say, we relit their lanterns for them, trimmed their wicks and allowed them the real communication. The communionists – I feel is the right word – no? They were in communion with the spirit again?'

'Yes. Nowadays a congregation would be made up of all sorts. There would be some people who would come because they disbelieved and they would want to jeer and that kind of stuff and there are those that get relit and there are those that hear the words but they don't actually put them into practice.'

'As you say, there were some that were beyond all hope, some who did not want to listen but just wanted to come and abuse.'

'What happened to them? Did they come back and have another go at that level?'

'I'm sure they would be coming back until they realised their mistakes and to be, I suppose, like we were, non-judgemental, again. They found it very difficult. But when I walked and went to different places, I never put my beliefs on anyone. They all came of their own free will, even those that came to jeer.'

'Did you have special techniques for dealing with those who came to jeer?'

'Just to ignore them, we did not have your modern-day guards to eject them from—'

'Bouncers?'

'That's the word, yes.'

'So being non-judgemental is very high on the list – live and let live?'

'Well, how can you live a life of being judgemental all the time?'

'Well, people do, though.'

'But what sort of lives do they have?'

'Pretty sad, because nobody measures up, because they don't know any better.'

'I am not saying that you should go through life and not pass judgement, because at times you must, but at times you must put your opinions across, and sometimes your opinions may be judgemental but again there is a balance between the two. There is being judgemental and judgemental, but judgemental spoken with a true heart is less judgemental than that spoken with spite.'

'Yes, you have to have a basic sense of morality and compassion. Compassion is the guide to keep you in the right frame of judgementalism. Non-judgementalism.'

'A perfect one for the ladies, maybe, if a friend bought a new dress and asked you your opinion and the dress was the most ugly thing you had seen in your life, would you turn round and say, "It looks like a potato sack on you"? Very harsh. Or would you be more gentle and say perhaps, "That is the wrong style for you, it doesn't suit you"? Two ways of being judgemental, you see, one spoken harshly and cruelly, the other is being gentle and truthful.'

'A very good example.'

'Not rules to live by, but things to think of, and is it not the old adage of thinking before you speak, but thinking as you speak. That is part of the way I was. Another example of being judgemental is if you saw a man or woman beating their donkey with a big stick, how would you approach this one?'

'Maybe ask them if you could help. That would be a good way to do it.'

'You would go in the reverse scenario of the first one. What I would have done would have gone and spoken to the person rather angrily.'

'Make them realise that what they were doing was not going to help.'

'Yes, of course, and there again judgemental when you need to be harsh, but it is coming from the heart again.'

'It is very difficult in that situation when someone is beating a poor little animal or a little child. I've always been worried that they are so insensitive that once I've told them off, they will take it out on the child even more. That's always a worry too because somehow—'

'That is the modern world now, from what I see.'

'Yes, and all the laws and regulations against interference and all that stuff. I had that the other day. A woman hit a small child and I nearly strangled her, you know? I almost hit her. I had no time for her at all.'

'And what did you do?'

'She was a bit far away, and with my condition I couldn't run after her at all and she disappeared down an alleyway. But I felt really angry. Can I ask you? You touched upon anger in the so-called "scriptures". I find I can see you actually demonstrated quite a lot of emotions, from compassion to anger too. Well, I don't know how right that is. But what was the general way in which you felt? Was it to do with you being enlightened, or was it the way you actually felt about life? Were you ever scared or frightened?'

'Of course, as I have said to you many times, I was only human flesh and blood. Kick me in the shins and they hurt as much as yours, and with the anger at times too, yes. It is in one of the scriptures that I overturned the money lenders' tables. How would you feel if you went to your spiritual gatherings and there were money lenders and people exchanging money there? Would you not feel that it had desecrated some of you and some of your space and something that you loved?'

'Yes, it cheapens it.'

'Yes. But then to have, I do not know your words of people in charge, to stand there watching and taking their cut and putting it in their pockets. Or in another way maybe, with all of you going to your local churches, how would you feel if the local bank had set up within the church? It would make you angry from inside. But there was no difference. I may not have been one to use churches and synagogues and the like, but I still had what you would call standards of behaviour of what you would expect.'

'Yes, a spiritual centre.'

'Again, another example to think of, you would not expect to go into a garrison barracks and find mass orgies and drinking rife. A different example perhaps, but exactly the same.'

'Inappropriate behaviour.'

'Yes, of course. I am not saying in your modern days this does not happen, but that is an example of seeing two sides of the coin which are the same.'

'Can you remember what your general life mood was, if there is such a thing? Were you joyous, because of what you knew? Were you content? Were you serene? These are all the sort of things that really interest me...how you actually felt.'

'I had good days and bad days, but in general, knowing the communications I could have and knowing that I was doing what I wanted to do, generally I was happy. There had been mood swings. An example of the time when I went to the wilderness, but this was just time for me. I know it has been written in the scriptures that the devil offered me the world, and maybe it did, but that was the devil within myself. I feel the modern-day term is fighting your demons and that was me fighting my demons of my doubt.'

'You had a crossroads. You had a choice of going two ways, and you had to quell the demon before you could carry on?'

'Yes, but my demon was the element of doubt. I doubted myself, my talents, even my friends. I'm sorry, you were going to speak, my friend.'

'I was going to say that it leads on to that other thing we were going to talk about, the studying that you did. When you were studying, was it with the intent of what you actually did afterwards? Did you feel that you had a specific aim, that you wanted to tell other people about what you had learned and was it like a passion that you really felt strongly about?'

'Many, many questions there.'

'Yes, I'm sorry.'

'Now coming back to the learning, or do you want me to finish the wilderness?'

'Yes, I'd like you to finish the wilderness.'

'That was just a special time for me, because again I had seen a crossroad in life and I just wanted to focus on my path, where I was going. So to move forward I had to cut away all element of doubt.'

'Could you have had no idea that things were going to get as severe as they did, the crucifixion and so on, at that point?'

'No idea at all.'

'So you were down to your own power to fulfil your purpose?'

'What purpose? The purpose that you have read in the Bible that I was supposed to fulfil?'

'No, your own purpose that you came with.'

'That was where my element of doubt was coming in. Was I doing this right, was I getting to the right people, and was I just the right person for the job. Exactly like all of you, I'm sure you have all been through doubtful times, either within a personal relationship or at work or even purchasing a home. It is just a part of being human, but again, many people forgot that I was human.'

'At that time?'

'Or at any time.'

'No, I mean, how many, and did people even then have greater expectations of you?'

'Only those jealous ones in authority.'

'Right, who feared you because of your power?'

'I did not have any power. They were the ones who thought I had power, but we all have power in our own way and in our own right.'

'So when you were in the wilderness, were you basically meditating and communicating with spirit and your guides and asking for guidance?'

'And just being quiet, which did open up many things for me and allowed me to understand my pathway more and to realise that I wasn't wasting my time and the world out there as I was seeing it. I do not mean to say it was mine for the taking, but it was there and I did not need any greed or any promises of unnamed wealth to venture into it. It was there, I suppose, to be rediscovered and to help even, as I would call them, modern man then, to rediscover themselves. There were no secrets from the past, as you all know now, you are rediscovering yourselves and your higher spiritual selves. This is exactly what I did, and it is some of this after the wilderness, that I put across to people.'

'What you are saying is a lot of the message that you got in the wilderness rekindled your inspiration?'

'Yes, that is a better way of putting it.'

'It reaffirmed what you already knew?'

'But, I suppose, in another way I had been giving so much and lighting so many candles for them, I had not realised that my work had come down to nothing and that needed retrimming. Does that sound a better way for you? Because, I am sure, as you all know, within this work you are doing, you always give to others and nine times out of ten you forget yourselves. So basically, that is what I did when I went to the wilderness. I had, I suppose, got lost, exhausted myself and just needed time to refuel.'

'I wonder what sort of age you were then. How long was it before things came to a crisis?'

'It wasn't very long.'

'Years?'

'A few years, but again, as you see, I was still a young man at the time. I'm not saying I wasn't a mature young man, but how many young men in your modern world now could you think of who would do what I did, or maybe doing exactly what you are doing now? One other question for you, if they did, what would the modern world think of them?'

'So you have to have a very clear picture of who you are in order to do that work, that is what you are saying, a clear picture of self?'

'Yes, but what would the modern man call a young man who did this work now?'

'A weirdo, mad.'

'Thank you, thank you. I wondered when somebody would come up with the answer. He would be classed as a nutcase.'

'At this same time, yes.'

'Why wasn't I classed as a nutcase, then?'

'Maybe you were.'

'More food for thought for you.'

'By some, by others who were ready to open up and wanted to—'

'Accept.'

'They would be open and accepting and I'm sure that there were others that were—'

'Just as closed as they are now, even more so maybe. So maybe those that were closed then are still the same ones that are closed now as our friend there said.'

'But I think it's important to have people around you who have similar goals, similar beliefs, in order to keep you—'

'Keep you afloat and keep you at a balance. But as I said before, the wilderness was only a time for me to readjust again. Maybe, I suppose, put my thoughts back into perspective and move forward with life again.'

'And Mary didn't come with you?'

'She couldn't have done, because I went on my own.'

'But she understood?'

'Mary encouraged me to go and have some time on my own to sort myself out.'

'Did she worry about you?'

'She didn't send me any mail. Yes, of course. She sent me off with a bag of herbs and things that I may need, or in your modern-day terms, a first aid kit.'

'I don't think we've touched on your journey into the wilderness and the time out, have we? Was it months?'

'It was about two maybe three weeks, a few days to get where I was going and settle myself in, and a few days to get back. It was one big wilderness. However, I wasn't very far off the mountains but I didn't go to the mountains because I wanted to be nearer for communication, so the wilderness was more convenient. I had shade and water and, of course, food. It wasn't very far from where we were, or where we had based ourselves.'

'What were your criteria for the wilderness? Was it so nobody could find you? Was that one of the main factors?'

'I just wanted, or needed, time for me. As I said earlier, maybe I had given so much over a period of time that I was mentally, physically and spiritually exhausted and I needed time to refill my tanks. I felt the more exhausted I got, the more angry I got – as you said earlier on, did I have emotions? – the more frustrated I

123

became. So it was the easiest thing to do, to take myself away. I know that Mary and the other few people with us had time on their own for their quiet contemplations and things. So it was not only for me, it was for the group as a whole. It was a little special time for each and every one of us who had given so much.'

'A holiday?'

'Yes, I suppose in that way of your modern terms, yes. Even though they were based not far from me, they still had their quiet special times.'

'When you say "they", how many are we talking about in your group at that time?'

'I would say eight, maybe nine.'

'Mary and the disciples?'

'Mary and my followers.'

'Where did the name or phrase "disciples" come from?'

'Where do you think?'

'The churches?'

'There you are.'

'And why was it thought that you had 12? One for each sign of the zodiac?'

'How many people do you have in a witches' coven?'

'Thirteen – oh, that's the churches again.'

'Well, they did crucify me in the end and try and prove me to be evil. But what's a better way of putting it? Manipulate the figures to suit themselves, which is something I feel hasn't changed, even in modern times.'

'But then the Church has used you to their advantage so that—'

'But why?'

'Once again, control, money, gain, so that where they might have said 12 in the beginning, and you 13, in order to make it sound negative, it's actually turned around, because they've used you for their own gain.'

'But it is their policy and their guilt.'

'I just wondered if this isn't too specific. Who were your followers at that time?'

'Does it matter?'

'I suppose it's just an interest in who were close to you.'

'All of them. There were one or two who wanted to stay in the local town or village when we went to the wilderness. I went a little bit further afield for myself. But again, please do not take all that has been written by the churches.'

'No, that's what we're trying to dispel, isn't it? I'm just aware that people have such very specific questions.'

'But there are specific questions you can ask back.'

'Like "what do you think?"'

'And who translated? And why did it take 100 to 150 years to write this story after my so-called death? And they call themselves religious. I feel they would not know the word if it were to bite them on the backside.'

'I'm trying to get a picture of what led up to this. You obviously worked so hard as a group, that you needed this time, this space, to heal and rebuild yourselves. So what did the rest do – was it basically you and Mary talking, healing, giving messages, or was everyone in the group doing the same thing?'

'They were doing similar, maybe not on such a deep level as myself and Mary, but they all had their own individual skills as well.'

'A bit like our current-day spiritual development circle where we help to bring them on.'

'Help them to meditate, even with the skills of healing. Some of them would change bandages and clean people up. It was not only the spiritual side, it was the physical side of life as well. In your modern day, doctors and nurses, I suppose. Some had skills of cooking better than others, some with skills of hunting when we were between villages and towns. As I said, we had to eat and drink as well.'

'You worked cooperatively.'

'It was like, I suppose, a mini moving community.'

'Can we move on from the wilderness now? Going to your studies and your aims when you were doing your studies, did you feel you wanted to take what you had learned out into the world, to help other people understand what you understood?'

'Yes. Why would you study to keep all the knowledge for yourselves, rather selfish, is it not?'

'It is, but people do. People that you learned from didn't go out and do that, people came to them.'

'No, but they taught just the same. I am not saying that I passed every scrap of knowledge that I had to others, but I passed on what I felt they would understand and what they needed, and some people needed more than others, some people did not need any at all. But I just wanted to go out and share my knowledge with those in the world who would appreciate it, and maybe even use some and maybe, they would pass their knowledge on to some others as well.'

'When you were doing this studying, did you have this view of yourself doing what you did?'

'I had thoughts of wanting to help those who were maybe unable to help themselves, yes. It wasn't in the way of making me lots and lots of money, it was just to share knowledge that had been hidden by the churches.'

'How did you make your money?'

'What money?'

'Well, when you fled, you had money to take with you then, enough to buy a smallholding, so that must have been quite a considerable amount of money.'

'Not in those days, no.'

'Enough to buy a smallholding and how did you—'

'Survive financially after that, you mean?'

'Not when you were in France, but before that. How did you get the money you took with you to buy the smallholding?'

'Some of the gold which had been given to me as a child by the wise men had been deposited or kept somewhere safe. It had been kept for a rainy day for me. Admittedly, my parents had used some of it with the upbringing of myself and my other siblings, but when it was found that I was moving on, it was reproduced and sent away with us. Again, it may not have been, in your modern terms lots and lots, but there was enough for us to survive for two or three years without working. As you know, we invested in a smallholding and I'm not saying that the money poured in from there, because it didn't, but it kept us and, in the end, we had what I would call a comfortable life, still doing what I was always prepared to do and with Mary, but maybe not on such a grand scale as what we had been. And the studies, there was maths, as we would call it, astrology, writing and languages.'

'And healing? And was it also meditation, or was that extra curricular?'

'That was more what I picked up in India when I went there. There was a small amount but you could write it on a small piece of paper. But what I learned in India was the real, full depth of meditation. Sorry, you were going to say, my friend?'

'No, I was adding, that was where you learned to remove your body and which in the end saved you.'

'I had heard of these things when I was studying in Greece, but the few masters or teachers there, were rather reluctant to pass this knowledge on. Reluctant because they were not frightened of losing the power of what they could do, but they were frightened of damaging people. Because, again, some of the speculation from our good friends, the churches, if you

127

leave your body, you will not be able to get back and your soul will be cast into the pits of hell.'

'So the Grecians actually had that influence on them?'

'Some of them, yes, but they were frightened of strangers like me, I suppose. But it is something that they did not pass on to many, and I do know that when they did, it was always to the older generation who were coming towards the end of their lives.'

'And you were a young whippersnapper?'

'Yes.'

'Were they frightened that it would come back on them?'

'I feel maybe there was a deeper side, yes.'

'So why were the Indians different? They could see more?'

'They were a more spiritual people.'

'So they could link with you on a higher level?'

'Yes.'

And think that you were the right person to give the knowledge to. It's a shame that the Grecians didn't do that. Were the people in India aware that you were coming?'

'Why should they be aware?'

'I don't know, since they were so spiritually advanced, I just wondered if they just had an inkling.'

'No.'

'And perhaps recognised you?'

'I feel maybe some of them might have done, but I suppose it was very low key, in your words. That is where I learned deep meditation. We would sit and fast and meditate for a week or maybe ten days in one session.'

'What made you decide to reincarnate in that particular area, when you were choosing what you were going to do prior to you reincarnating? What were the factors that made you decide you had to go down there?

Was it to do with the corruption of spirituality in that area?'

'Yes.'

'So you could have easily gone to India?'

'I could have gone to anywhere, yes. It was a chosen goal, might be the right words to use. To help those who needed the help. If I had gone to India at that time, would they have needed my help? They were a very advanced race of people.'

'That life of yours caused huge repercussions all over the world and still does. Do you feel that you fulfilled what you actually wanted to do?'

'Until the crucifixion, yes, and then after that, you could say that my career was cut short.'

'But then you've had an everlasting effect on the world since that time and presumably that is something you didn't expect.'

'But I haven't had an everlasting effect on the world.'

'The Church has caused you to have an everlasting effect on the world.'

'Ah, but how many years did it take before they realised, 150 years after my death?'

'It has been a long time since then and you are the pinnacle of the so-called Christian Church throughout the world.'

'But why? Should they not hang their heads in shame?'

'They should do, yes.'

'Why should I be strung up on a cross for you to come and say, "Oh, that's nice, thank you"? I would be thoroughly ashamed to crucify someone and then use them as a figurehead.'

'Had it not been for this, we would never have met you, so there are good things that happen.'

'Good things, yes.'

'Well, I think that the Church uses that to make us flagellate ourselves at Easter, it perpetuates the guilt, doesn't it?'

'But why Easter?'

'Because that is when it was reported that you had been crucified.'

'They picked on that time because it was a Pagan festival – Esotori.'

'What was that?'

'Esotori – Easter – a big Pagan festival for the beginning of the fertility of the land, and what better time to control the masses again? It is the same whichever part of the world you look at. They all have a special time at what you call Easter.'

'So with this book that we are going to write with the truth in it, I mean, there are obviously going to be people that are going to be very deeply upset with what's been written, because it's going to shake their—'

'Beliefs to the rotten core. But again, my friend, may I just cut you short, sorry, but are you forcing them to buy and read your book?'

'No.'

'It is their freedom of choice. At least with your book, you will not be like the churches and forcing your beliefs on others.'

'No. But I think there will be people that will agree with it and there will be people who won't. I think, that this world is an ever-changing world and that the churches are losing their control and that little by little, this, and lots of other things, are helping the Church to actually lose its grip on that "greatness" that they have had for so long. And I say "greatness" in inverted commas.'

'Thank you. I would not call it greatness, I would call it greed.'

'Greed, yes, but they've pumped themselves up to be something wonderful, by which a lot of people have fallen under their spell, as it were. I think there have been more challenges to the Church this year than ever.'

'They have, from what I have seen from my realms, brought it upon themselves.'

'What would you say to churchgoers nowadays who, in all humility and all belief, follow what has been set down for them. It's not their fault that they have been sold a pup, as such, and yet they are good people, they follow the way that is shown to them. What would you say to them?'

'Baaaa.' Laughter.

'Quite a good answer, really. That's their crime, isn't it, that they haven't thought for themselves? They have good hearts.'

'They have good hearts but they have not—'

'They have been conned.'

'As our friend said, they are sheep.'

'That's the line they sell – I am the good shepherd, you know.'

'But why do sheep have to follow a shepherd? Was the shepherd not there to keep them safe and look after them, not to lead them by the nose?'

'I know a few people, monks, who are such good people, and yet the message that they have been told is totally wrong. That's the message they have swallowed. It's their choice to listen to the message and not think it through, but with this judgemental thing, it doesn't make them any lesser people does it?'

'No, no, my friend, but who is being judgemental towards them? Not you in your book. You are just saying, this is what we have. As when I preached and, I do not mean it that way, but when I talked and spoke to people, it was their choice whether they took my beliefs or walked away. I did not force them upon them. When

131

you go into churches and the ministries, you have to promise to do the will of the God in the way that they teach, and that is, being led by the nose.'

'Yes, of course. I just wanted to say that these people we are talking about, they actually do follow a very good moral code because, set down in the Bible, whether you believe it or whether you don't, there is a set of moral rules which, if everybody followed, this world would be a much better place. All right, it's come from a different source, but still, these people may be misguided in their actual belief, as you have explained to us. Nevertheless, you must give it to them, that they are trying to follow a decent moral code.'

'I've always looked upon it as the singer and not the song. You know, it's the good person, not the actual belief. Just look around, there are about 100, more than 100, different beliefs available, so, if you're a good man—'

'Yes, I'm not saying these people are wrong, but it would be entirely up to them what they chose.'

'Isn't it a lot to do with availability? What is available to the average man at the time? I knew nothing about what we do now when I was ten years old.'

'Yes, yes. When I was a child I thought as a child, now I am a man, or a woman.'

'Very difficult.'

'But it comes through generations, doesn't it, the beliefs and our families? So it's almost set in stone in many ways. That is why it is very hard to forget what you were brought up with. We even spoke a little bit about that last time, when I spoke about what you used to teach, not teach—'

'Talk about, then.'

'With the children in schools and how the fact that all the community was of a similar sort of open-minded belief. Therefore, that generation of children would be much more open-minded than your current generation, so you do have a big influence on children and bringing them up. So you are right. It is about what we learn – indoctrination.'

'A perfect question to ask, maybe, or for all of you to ask when this book comes out and people are putting you down or the churches are up in arms. Ask them, do you not believe in the Holy Spirit and communication? One – what is the Holy Spirit, and two – why is it only ordained priests and vicars that have this so-called ability to communicate with the Holy Spirit? So, before you complain to us about what we are saying in here, could you please answer these two questions for me? There is no difference. Ask them – what is the Holy Spirit, then?'

'What it says in the book, that's what it is.'

'Ask them for their own interpretation, then.'

'Constantly referring to the book.'

'No references to books, please.'

'That is the thing about the Bible, isn't it, that it has been used?'

'How many times has the Bible been translated into different languages? A perfect one is your King John's.'

'King James's.'

'King James's Bible. He wrote in the Bible what he wanted, so again it makes it—'

'It's lovely prose, but not to build a life upon. That's exactly what my mother would say when I questioned it, "but it's a lovely piece of poetry".'

'Rather than seeing the Bible as a holy book, see it as diary from history and take what is relevant for you and discard the rest.'

'I would like to ask your opinion on something. You are regarded as a prophet, whatever that means. There were many prophets before you, as the book says. Now, what about Mohammed? Are you in communication with Mohammed?'

'In the spirit realms, yes, we are all on the same level.'

'I would love to know whether the Koran was an inspiration, or was it like the spirit teachings that we have. How did it actually come down, if it ever did? I can't read it in the original, but they say it is a transcendently beautiful and hermetic message. Can you just give us a couple of sentences on that?'

'I will do my best. From what I know now from the spirit realms, the Koran is, or was, spiritual teachings which were channelled. I will not say it laid out rules for living, but this for them was a simple way of trying to live a spiritual life, in the best way that they could. But again, many things in books and other things have been changed – one or two things have been tinkered with to—'

'Suit, yes, I understand that. Like, I should think, the Ten Commandments. Is the Koran on the same sort of line as the Ten Commandments, to teach the people how to live a clean and safe life at that time?'

'Yes, it is just a way of trying, not to keep people in order, but to bring them back from the brink of self-destruction. Not rules that you've got to literally strictly live your life by, no, but as guidelines to assist you in trying to live a decent life, if that is the right word.'

'And the Koran has been misinterpreted as much as the other scriptures, I assume.'

'Misinterpretation and complete distortion. People translating rather than word for word, but translating and thinking, "Ah, that is what they want, that is what they meant", so they are supposing.'

'I think you mean transforming.'

'No, I think they were translating, but putting their own translation on what they had.'

'The Koran cites you as a prophet. I take it you have no objection to that?'

'None at all!'

'Good.'

'When you are walking the earth, you are all entitled to your opinions. I didn't see myself as a prophet, but that is something I had to come to terms with and understand over a period of time.'

'But you are a master, are you not? Does that not rank higher than a prophet?'

'Words for control again.'

'But all of it is about the fact that you are an evolved being. So, whether you put the name of prophet, master or rogue...'

'Master, prophet, rogue – I've got three titles – sorry!'

'You are an evolved being.'

'And are you not all sitting round this table evolved beings as well?'

'Yes, yes, we are all equal, but some are more equal than others. The Koran says that Mohammed is the last prophet. I always understood that he was the latest prophet in the line, but the Muslims claim that there is no other prophet after him, and yet we all in this room are prophets to a certain degree, are we not?'

'Yes.'

'And that's what I find—'

'Very difficult!'

'And to score as a prophet, you've got to really do big things. But that's not true, is it?'

'No.'

'We all have that potential. Well, it's the same as mediums, we are all mediums. But to score as a medium you've got to be recognised by a lot of people as doing something wonderful, and it's not all our aim to do that, is it?'

'So there you are, words again, my friend.'

'I understood St Paul to be an evolved being. He must have lived to about the same year as you, he must have been about the same age. And he had this point of revelation didn't he, where he was struck blind? Though, I imagine, at that point, you must have been in France. What interests me is that he had a blinding flash from God, or felt that he did, and then became what he thought was a prophet, wrote to the apostles and spent the rest of his life trying to convert people.'

'Why should he want to convert people? They were happy how they were.'

'Exactly.'

'It goes against the grain exactly of what I was doing.'

'Absolutely, so I was just wondering if you were aware of him because he was picking up on the rumours about your life, which had, by then, been written down and he walked around telling everyone, or converting them. Are you aware of any of that? Oh, you are not.'

'It takes all sorts to make a world, and as you know, if there is one group of people doing good, how many other people jump on the bandwagon to cash in to make themselves look good. Why would he want to convert people, convert them from what, and what would he convert them to?'

'Christianity, apparently.'

'But there wasn't Christianity when I was about. It was a modern word put on by the churches.'

'The Bible says – so it must be right – you were their main topic of his conversations.'

'Yes, a bit like your medium friend, D**** A****, jumping on the bandwagon, cashing in on everybody else.'

'That's what you feel about him?'

'Why would this man want to convert people to Christianity? Cannot they be happy with what they are?

He is being as bad as the churches for herding people in one place and keeping them there. Control again.'

'Well, he was so inspired that he wanted to become a dealer, a dealer in religion. Get some of what I've got. It's quite a human trait.'

'A "freeloader" in your modern terms.'

'Can I ask a question?'

'Yes.'

'Was there actually ever anything physically known as the Holy Grail?'

'There was a cup or bowl which we had at the last supper, yes.'

'And that is what is known as the Holy Grail?'

'What my favourite people put on it, yes.'

'Your favourite people?'

'The churches!'

'So, I presume this Holy Grail no longer exists?'

'Well, how long would a piece of a clay bowl last?'

' Not too long, I wouldn't have thought.'

'I know there have been many geological finds, but that is all it was, only a clay bowl which we shared a last toast with.'

'So it relates symbolically to that cup? I don't know, I'm asking.'

'Again, what you have been indoctrinated to believe.'

'There had been many quests for the Holy Grail, why has that happened, is it just greed again?'

'Yes.'

'What led people to believe that certain others have got the Holy Grail?'

'Greed again and jealousy. I know we have individuals here, but as each individual, how would you have seen the Holy Grail, before I had told you what it was?'

'Quite different, quite different.'

'How would you have seen it?'

Jesus now speaks to individual members of the group.

Group member 1: 'Well, I would have seen it just as a metal bowl not necessarily gold.'

'Okay, and our friend?'

Group member 2: 'I would have seen it in exactly the same way.'

Group member 3: 'I have never attached any importance to it whatsoever.'

'Well done.'

Group member 4: 'I don't know what to say, I have a childhood memory of being taught that it was a golden cup.'

'A golden cup encrusted with jewels?'

'Yes.'

'But where would a poor lad like me get a golden cup encrusted with jewels? Wishful thinking and, again, coming back to our favourite subject, trying to make themselves better, and look what we've got. I know there have been many quests for it.'

'So you're saying that they made their own Holy Grail this ornate piece of—'

'Yes, where would I have got jewels and gold from in my lifetime, as you have heard over the past few weeks, unless I had robbed some rich Turkish sultan of all his gold and jewels?'

'I didn't realise that there was actually—'

'It was only a small cup or a bowl in which we shared, in your modern terms again, a glass of wine.'

'It's a red herring, isn't it, attaching something important to something that was everyday and mundane?'

'Yes, even with washing my hands. It was the done thing. You wash your hands even in modern times before you serve food, do you not? So, we all washed our hands because we ate with our fingers. And coming back to the Holy Grail, my friend, there had been many quests to look for it, yes, but they all seemed to be looking on the physical rather than meditating and going to the spirit realms. There had only been one, and I cannot think of his name, one of King Arthur's knights.'

'Lancelot?'

'No, I cannot think of the knight's name, but he was the only one that basically, I think he had, not a serious accident, but he had a rather nasty crack on the head and he was unconscious for a few days and he had actually seen the Grail when his spirit had gone to the spirit realms to be healed.'

'But he told Arthur that he was wasting his time.'

'That it was not physical, yes, so, he is the only one that I know of that has realised. Many others are after it because they think it is a gold encrusted cup, full of priceless jewels.'

'Worth a lot of money! What about the fact that the Catholics, the Catholic Church, thought that the Cathars had got the Holy Grail when they were holed up in their castle on Montségur?'

'Greed. And what better way to work them out than with an excuse to go in and do it?'

'But it's said that five Cathars escaped with—'

'Some secret.'

'Yes. So was that anything to do with the Holy Grail, or was it something else?'

'It was a document.'

'And the document, are we allowed to know what that is?'

'It was just a family tree.'

'Yours?'

'That will become plain later maybe. It was just a document with a family tree and a few words on how to get a clearer communication with the spirit realms.'

'Is the document still in existence?'

'I don't think it is. If it is, it may still be buried somewhere, but it would be very fragile now.'

'Is the information that was on the document still recorded somewhere?'

'That I do not know.'

'Okay. Thank you. But nobody's ever seen the Holy Grail, have they?'

'If it is not physical, how can you see it? Only in, as I say, meditation and again, if it were shown to you in meditation, would it be shown to you in the way that you could understand and grasp it?'

'Doesn't it mean a symbol of attainment or finding some truth?'

'But again, if you meditate and, we will say you see the Grail, you are finding the truth, but the truth does not exist on the physical plane. I do not wish to sound facetious, my friend, but once you have seen that, it will open up many doors for you, especially during meditation and doing other spiritual things.'

'I wish they had said "cup" in the first place, because I never knew what it was until seeing some film about Indiana Jones or something. I had no idea what it meant. I'd heard it, but I didn't understand.'

'I'm curious about the Old Testament, how things have linked with the Old Testament, but that was—'

'That was before my time.'

'But I'm thinking about the religious side, the Biblical side, how that had been brought through really, people's beliefs. But I don't know how far you had gone.'

'But who was one of the greatest mediums in the Old Testament?'

'Moses? Elijah?'

'Jacob as well.'

'Abraham?'

'I know they were supposed to make a sacrifice, but did they not all talk to God, or the Great Spirit, or whatever words you use. Did they not all have the ability to do this? They were never reviled and drummed away like you are now.'

'I like what you said about the scriptures being a diary, a diary of a people.'

'You see it as a diary and you see it in a different light, then.'

'And anything else has been twisted.'

'I would love to interview your mother. I would really enjoy that, would that be possible?'

'Maybe it's time for a meditation, my friend, or to ask in your dreams.'

'Yes, I'll try that.'

'It'll take a few times to get the link, but I am sure she would be only too willing to speak.'

'There is a lot of myth that needs to be dispelled around her. I wouldn't mind getting it from the horse's mouth, as such.'

'Yes, I understand, my friend – ask, I am sure she will accommodate as and when she can. Again, like you, how many people have asked?'

'I don't know at all.'

'There you are. I presume you have completed your questions?'

'I think we need to ask if we can have another session after we have brought all this together.'

'Of course you can, my friend, as I say.'

'We can't assume that.'

'And why not?'

'Why not? Because you're in the chair, you might be doing other things.'

'I will always make special time for my special friends.'

General thanks.

'May I say to you all thank you for your patience and your time? Bless you all and take care.'

Chapter Six

The Final Word

'Blessings, my friends, and how can I help you today?'

'We would like to know what you think about what we have done so far with the book. Whether there is anything particularly that is missing or whether there is anything else that you have thought about that needs to go in, or any changes. Also, what you are hoping to gain from what we are doing? What the reason is for us doing this and what do you expect the outcome to be?'

'Well, hopefully for the myth to be put away, about myself. Admittedly I was in some way someone supposedly important, but I was never sent here to assist you with your sins. How I died on the cross for your sins, even though I died 2,000 years before you were born, what an utter shambles, is that the right phrase for your modern times?'

'That is something that the churches have concocted, isn't it?'

'Again, as I have spoken through this one many times saying about the control of the religions. I would like to see people enlightened to bring together the world as one again, because far too much has been done in my name or for the sake of me or the person they call my father. I still find it very confusing that they are fighting a war for the good of God. Is God not good anyway?'

'What I think you are trying to do is to normalise yourself as a normal human being that had to go through living as all of us have to do on earth and that you didn't want the elevated position that you were given posthumously, maybe even while you were alive, but posthumously I would think is more relevant.'

'Yes, posthumously is more relevant. I was like a similar strain of all of you. I had clairvoyant talents, which I have said many times, and healing talents, which you all have, but it did not make me any more special than anyone else.'

'I think from what I have been reading and what is recorded, that you had a great facility for accessing the other "stuff", and as you say we all have, but it is to a lesser degree than you, and maybe it is what the world needed at the time.'

'I suppose in a way, that I had an access, as you say, into the extra abilities to channel energies to turn things around for the good, or to use them for the good.'

'Yes, what the old scriptures call prophet, but we now know that it is a human condition and can be accessed by anyone.'

'Yes, an ability that I have heard this one say many times, that we all have, but it is down to us as individuals as to whether we tap into and use these abilities. Like yourselves, you have chosen to step along the pathway of being able to tap into a deeper source, and if I can say so, a more pure source of energy, to heal and to help people to communicate.'

'How do you feel about the almost finished book that we have now put together?'

'From what I have seen from our side, it is very pleasing that you have kept to the spoken word from all of us. You have not veered from the pathway or filled in blanks that you thought would be appropriate, or taken things out because it is not correct in modern terms.'

'So you are happy that we go ahead with the finished product?'

'Yes, please. As long as you are all happy within yourselves.'

'Well, I sat down and read it having not read it for some months, and it struck me as "Wow! This is wonderful!" and I knew all about it!'

'But, is the book going to be one of these books that you read today and put it down and read again in six or nine months time and you read a deeper insight into times around me? Maybe even the third and fourth time you read again and peel back the different layers of the different aspects of things.'

'That's what we wanted to clear with you.'

'Can we ask, in your later years, in France, did you at one time remove your beard?'

'Yes.'

'Before you spoke to us were you showing yourself without that beard? Alan's face is quite tanned, but you looked darker tanned.'

'Yes. My beard was never wild, it was always neatly trimmed.'

'Was there a reason why you removed it? Was it part of your disguise?'

'I just wanted a change, no religious reasons either.'

'It must have been seen as very unusual because most men wore beards, and the longer and shaggier the better!'

'But I never liked them long and shaggy.'

'In the texts you use phrases that are anachronistic, in other words they are after your time, like "jumping the gun". Are you talking in our terms, is that what that is about?'

'Yes.'

'A lot of terminology does actually come from the present. If you were talking in the colloquial of the time we wouldn't understand you at all, so that's why. The other thing that I wanted to clear up was that you used the word "church". As far as I know "church" was an invention by the religion that was after you, in your name, is that the same?'

'Yes, using it as in the modern phrase for the masses now to understand. Even with going to France, which as you know would have been called Gaul, but to use that now, people would have said, "Where in the world is that?" So I have tried to use some of the terms that I have heard in the modern times to clarify things for the uneducated.'

'Yes. So to mean places of worship, temples, synagogues, that sort of thing?'

'Yes, but if you wish to change it, then please do.'

'No, I think that what we have just said will clarify that.'

'I was trying to talk in modern terms for the uninitiated or the uneducated.'

'Can we talk about the cover of the book, please? We haven't settled on that yet. We have got some artwork, have you viewed them?'

'There is some very nice artwork there, yes.'

'Are you able to "see" them?'

'That is the younger you with a covering over your head. That is a sad you, and that has got the thorns on your head.'

There is now a conversation where Jesus selects one of the pictures for the front and one for the back of the book.

'Have you actually perused the finished article and are you happy with it?'

'Yes, I have trusted you all, and that is why you were chosen for this task.'

'That is very comforting, thank you.'

'How many other people in the world would have accepted me coming through to speak and putting your trust in me for me to trust you to go forward with things?'

'I remember before all this started, you had come through and we had to come up to you one by one and promised that we would do something but we didn't know what we were promising. Each one of us put our hands between yours and said that we would do as you wished and then sat down and you said, "Well, I never, you have all made a promise and you don't even know what you have promised!" We said that we trusted you and, of course, this is what we had promised to do, this book, and we are so proud and privileged to be involved in this. Thank you from the bottom of our hearts.'

'It is a pleasure to come and speak through this one and converse with you all.'

'Perhaps we may have to call on you again when the flack gets too much and we need your advice.'

'The flack, as you say, will come from those who are afraid of the truth, afraid that their empire is crumbling.'

'There will always be those that will argue that you are wrong, that you are a crazy bunch.'

'Well, I don't mind that, most people think we are anyway, we are used to that.'

'I have heard this one say many times, if those in the religious sectors think you are barmy, what makes them think that they are sane? They profess to talk to God, so why can you not talk to me? But to me, what a sad controlling bunch, that they have got it into their heads that I was crucified to save their sins and what makes them think that the Bible is true? How many times has the Bible been translated? Did not King James write his own Bible, the way that he thought it should be written? If that makes a true story, why cannot ours be true, which we know in our hearts is true?'

'Well, we always talk about you as JC, and I know you don't mind, it seems more approachable somehow.'

'Why should I not be again? Those tales that I was superhuman, it was exactly the way I was when I walked the earth. I'm not saying that I tried to be friends with everyone, because it's something in this world that you cannot do, but I tried my best to help people the best way I could. I know that I was radical in the way that I spoke and I worked but I worked from my heart, like you all do, and I just wanted to do the best for mankind as I knew mankind. Not so much from the four corners of the earth but what I knew as my world at the time. I know that I had travelled to many different countries, but I saw my world as what was around me at the time.'

'Will there be a follow up book from you?'

'Maybe, yes. We will let the dust settle first!'

'JC Rides Again!' Laughter.

'Thanks to you all and please take my blessings. Go in peace.'